The Usborne Complete Book of ART ideas

Fiona Watt

Designed and Illustrated by
Antonia Miller, Non Figg, Katrina Fearn and Amanda Barlow

Additional design and illustration by Jan McCafferty, Lucy Parris, Nicola Butler, Natacha Goransky, Cristina Adami, Rachel Wells, Felicity House, Kathy Ward and Vici Leyhane

Photographs by Howard Allman

Americanization: Carrie Armstrong

Contents

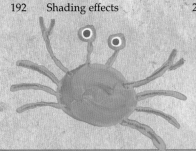

ART

ideas

Art materials

The ideas in this book use materials that are easy to find in any store that sells art supplies. These pages give you general information about art materials. You'll find out more on pages 100-101 and 196-197. Look on page 6 for information about brushes.

Paper

Under the heading on some pages, there is a suggestion of the type of paper to use. A few of the projects suggest bristol paper (a thick paper) or watercolor paper. You can buy these in books or in single sheets.

Bristol paper is good for using with inks and pastels.

Typing, computer print-out or newsprint paper

Watercolor paper is special paper for watercolors.

Pastel paper or Ingres paper is special paper for pastels.

Tissue paper

Keep clean

Before you start, protect the surface you're working on with lots of newspaper. Put on an old shirt or apron to protect your clothes, too.

Experiment with using different kinds of paper, such as brown wrapping paper.

Remember, if you use colored paper, the colors you put on it will change.

Paints

The type of paints used in this book are acrylic paint, watercolor paint, ready-mix and poster paint. They come in a variety of forms, such as dry blocks, tubes and bottles. See page 8 for some ideas of colors to buy.

The introduction to each section tells you how to mix that type of paint.

Acrylic paints come in tubes or bottles. Buy small tubes to begin with.

Watercolor blocks are more economical to use than tubes.

Ready-mix and poster paints are similar to acrylics but are cheaper.

You can get gold and silver acrylic and poster paint.

Inks

Colored inks come in small bottles. Use them with a brush or a dip pen for painting or drawing.

You can get ink cartridges in lots of colors.

Inks come in lots of very bright colors.

Pastels

There are ideas in this book which use chalk pastels and oil pastels. They are usually sold as a boxed set, but you can buy them individually.

Chalk pastels

Oil pastels give you much brighter colors than chalk pastels.

Wax crayons

Wax crayons usually come in sets. They aren't expensive and you can do some exciting things with them.

Pens

You will need a pen for some of the ideas in this book. You can also use an ordinary ink pen, cartridge pen or dip pen for drawing.

Felt-tip pen

Use a dip pen with ink in a bottle.

Cartridge pen

Other equipment

For some of the projects you may also need paper towels, old newspapers, a kitchen sponge, an old rag for wiping your brushes, yogurt containers and a large jam jar or plastic container for water.

Palettes

You will need something to mix your paints on. You don't need to have a mixing palette; use an old plate or a lid from a plastic container instead.

Use a white plate or lid. It will give you a good idea of the color you are mixing.

5

Brushwork

It's not essential that you use artists' paintbrushes for the ideas in this book, but you will find that they are easy to use and will give you some very good results.

Types of brushes

Paintbrushes come in a variety of types and sizes. Some brushes have soft bristles. These are good for using with inks and watercolors. Hard-bristled brushes are good for using with acrylics.

The soft bristles of this brush are sable, a type of animal hair. They are very good, but expensive.

Round-ended brushes

The number on a brush indicates its thickness. Size 4 is good for painting fine detail; size 12 for painting large areas.

Use a household paintbrush for backgrounds.

These two blue brushes have hard bristles.

Flat-ended brushes give you wide brushstrokes.

Brushstrokes

Different types of brushes make different marks, or 'brushstrokes'. You can also use the same brush to give you a variety of effects.

All these lines were made with a no. 5 brush.

For fine lines, use the tip of a brush. Press harder to get thicker lines.

Brushstrokes using light, then heavy pressure, on the brush

Taking care of brushes

 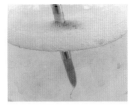 

Store brushes in a box or upright in a mug.

Don't leave brushes standing in water. This will damage the bristles.

Wash brushes in warm, soapy water. Hot water loosens the bristles.

Re-shape the bristles with your fingers before they dry.

Store brushes in a safe place where the bristles won't get damaged.

Build up patterns with different combinations of brushstrokes.

Lay the bristles flat on the paper, to make marks like these.

This checkerboard pattern was made with the tip of a flat-ended brush.

Use the tip of a fine, round brush to make small marks.

Dip pen

Chinese lettering brush

Feathers

Other 'brushes'

Piece of sponge

Cotton swabs

There are lots of other things, apart from artists' brushes that you can use to paint with. Experiment with some of the things shown here.

Mixing colors

You only need a few colors of paint to be able to mix a wide range of other colors. If you are going to buy some paints, here is a suggestion of the basic colors to get.

Ultramarine blue - good for mixing with red to make purples.

Lemon yellow - good for mixing with blue to make greens.

Yellow ochre - good for mixing with red to make earthy colors such as brown and terracotta.

Vermilion red - good for mixing with yellow to make orange, or with blue to make brown.

Prussian or cobalt blue - good for mixing with yellow to make greens.

Crimson red - good for mixing with blue to make purples.

Burnt umber - mix it with blue, to get black.

White - mix it with colors to make pastel shades.

Black and gray

These paints have been darkened with black.

This blue/brown mix has been added to crimson.

You don't need black to make gray, either.

If you mix black with a color to make it darker, the paint can look very dull. Use other colors instead to darken colors.

Instead of using black, mix ultramarine and burnt umber together. Mix in this blackish color to darken paints.

To mix a light gray, mix blue, with white, then add a tiny amount of yellow and vermilion.

Mixing colors for skies

Blue and white

Vermilion and lemon yellow

A little orange added.

More blue added.

A little white added.

Lots more blue, red and yellow added.

Add more white.

1. Mix white and blue on your palette. Clean your brush. Mix a little vermilion and lemon yellow to make orange.

2. Add a tiny amount of the orange to the blue you have mixed. See what color it makes. Then, try adding a little white.

3. Add different colors to the paint. Some of the colors would be good for a bright sunny sky, others for stormy skies.

Mixing skin colors

Brush the paint next to the square.

Match the colors as closely as you can.

1. Find pictures of faces in magazines. Cut a square from each one. Glue them onto paper.

2. Add some red paint to white, then a little yellow and blue, until you've got a good match.

3. Cut out half a face from a magazine and glue it onto paper. Paint the other half, matching the colors.

Mixing greens

You may have noticed that there is no green paint in the list of recommended colors. You don't need to buy it because you can easily use other colors to mix different greens.

1. Mix together a little yellow with blue to make a bright green color.

2. Then, add different amounts of red. See how many different greens you can make.

Acrylic paints

Acrylic paints are very bright and easy to mix. They can be used in a variety of ways to get different effects.

Using acrylics

Squeeze small blobs of acrylic paint onto an old plate or palette. Mix them with water, or use them straight from the tube. Wash your brushes well, because the paint is waterproof when it dries.

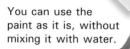

You can use the paint as it is, without mixing it with water.

Or, you can add water to the paint to make it thinner and more transparent.

Different effects

Using paint straight from the tube, try short brushstrokes with a flat-ended brush.

Paint a patch of color in thick paint, then scratch into it with a piece of cardboard.

Cut notches in a piece of cardboard. Scrape it across the paint to make lines.

Use the pointed end of a paintbrush to scratch swirls into thick paint.

For a criss-cross effect, press the edge of a piece of thick cardboard into the paint.

To get a textured pattern, scratch into thick paint with the prongs of a plastic fork.

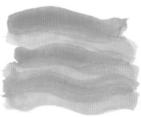

Mix paint with a little water to make it watery. Do wavy lines in different colors.

Paint lines with watery paint. Let them dry. Add shapes with thick paint on top.

This picture was created using papers decorated with patterns made in thick paint, using the techniques shown on the opposite page. Shapes were cut, then glued together to make a collage.

Thick and thin paint

THICK PAPER, SUCH AS BRISTOL PAPER

You can get different effects by using acrylic paint straight from a bottle or tube, or by thinning it with water. Acrylics also have an adhesive quality, so thin paper, such as tissue paper, sticks to it when the paint dries.

The background of the picture below was painted with thin paint, then patterns were added with thick paint.

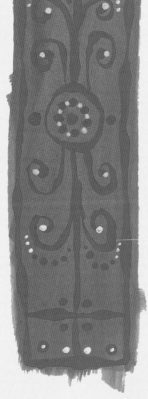

For a plaid pattern, the green and white stripes were painted with thin paint; the purple ones with thick paint.

The squares above were outlined with thin paint. Details were added with thick paint.

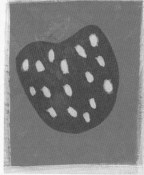

The purple flower on the right is tissue paper. Thick white paint was added on top.

Squares, lines and dots of thick paint

The strawberry was cut from tissue paper. Thin white paint was painted on top.

Tissue paper prints

Red or orange tissue paper work best.

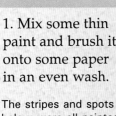

1. Mix some thin paint and brush it onto some paper in an even wash.

2. Cut a shape from tissue paper. Press it on the wet paint.

3. Leave the shape for a minute or so, then peel off the tissue paper.

The stripes and spots below were all painted with thick paint.

The top and bottom hearts were printed.

The flower and leaf on the left are tissue paper with thick paint on top.

The details on the dog and the fish were added with a felt-tip pen, once the paint had dried.

A tissue paper heart with thick paint on top.

Patterns and dots

LARGE PIECE OF BRISTOL PAPER

Mix the paints in a plastic container.

1. Mix red and yellow acrylic paints to make orange, then add blue to make rust.

2. Paint a large piece of paper all over with the rust paint. Use a thick paintbrush.

3. When the rust paint has dried, paint a large black snake curling around the paper.

4. Use yellow ochre to paint a circle in the middle of the snake. Let it dry.

5. Cut a piece of sponge cloth for the bottom of three more containers. Dampen the cloths.

6. Spread the sponge cloths with some black, ochre and white paint.

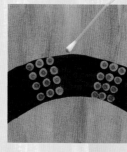

7. Press a cotton swab onto the ochre sponge. Print lines of dots on the snake.

8. Use another cotton swab to fill in between the lines with rows of rust dots.

9. Add white dots around the outline of the snake. Space the dots evenly.

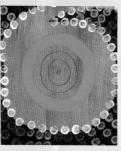

10. Draw circles inside the ochre one. Use these as guides to print white dots.

11. Print black and white flowers around the ochre circle. Fill in with ochre dots.

12. Print white and ochre flowers around the snake. Fill the background with black dots.

Glue pictures
A PIECE OF CARDBOARD

This idea uses household glue for drawing, which leaves a raised line when it dries. The raised lines are then covered with gold acrylic paint, and black shoe polish is rubbed in to get an 'antique' look.

You will need a bottle of household glue that has a nozzle top.

Test it on newspaper.

1. If the glue is new, snip a little piece off the nozzle. Test it to see the thickness of the line it makes.

2. If the line you have drawn is very thin, snip a little bit more off the end of the nozzle.

3. Draw a simple picture on the cardboard. Place the nozzle of the glue where you want to start.

4. Then, draw around your picture, squeezing the glue out gently as you draw.

5. When you get to the end of a line, lift the glue up quickly, so that it doesn't drip.

6. Add some wavy lines, swirls and dots on the cardboard, around your drawing.

7. Leave it to dry overnight. Then, paint all over with gold acrylic paint. Let the paint dry.

8. To get the antique look, put some black shoe polish on a soft cloth, then rub it all over.

Cut the cardboard
into different
shapes, before
decorating it.

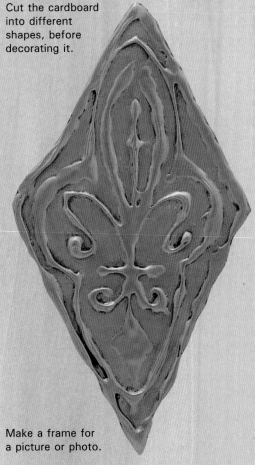

Make a frame for
a picture or photo.

Printing patterns

ANY PAPER

Use an old birthday card or postcard.

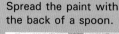
Spread the paint with the back of a spoon.

Press firmly.

1. Draw a simple shape on a piece of cardboard. Cut it out.

2. Press a lump of poster tack onto the back, to make a handle.

3. Squeeze paint onto newspaper. Spread the paint with a spoon.

4. Press the shape into the paint, then print it on some paper.

Printing patterns

Experiment with making different patterns. Try printing rows or joining up the prints.

Press the cardboard into the paint before you do each print.

Two-tone prints

Cut different shapes and print them as part of your pattern.

For a two-tone print, spread two colors of paint on the newspaper.

Press the shape into the paint where the two colors meet.

Straight lines

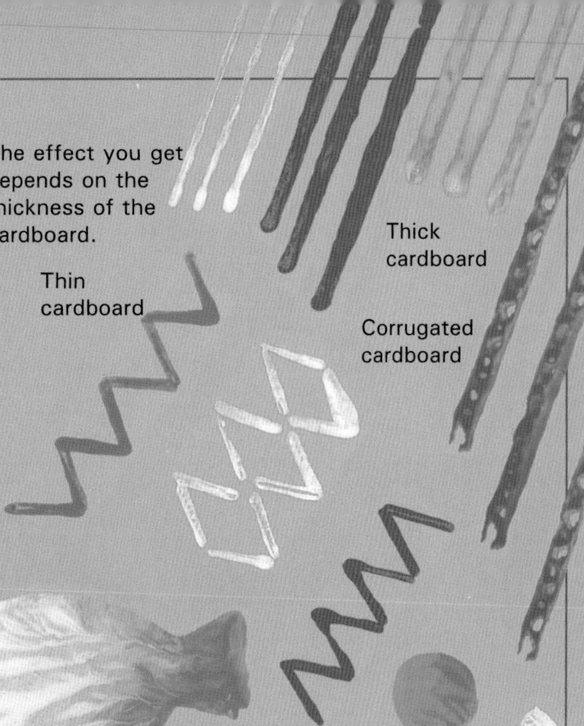

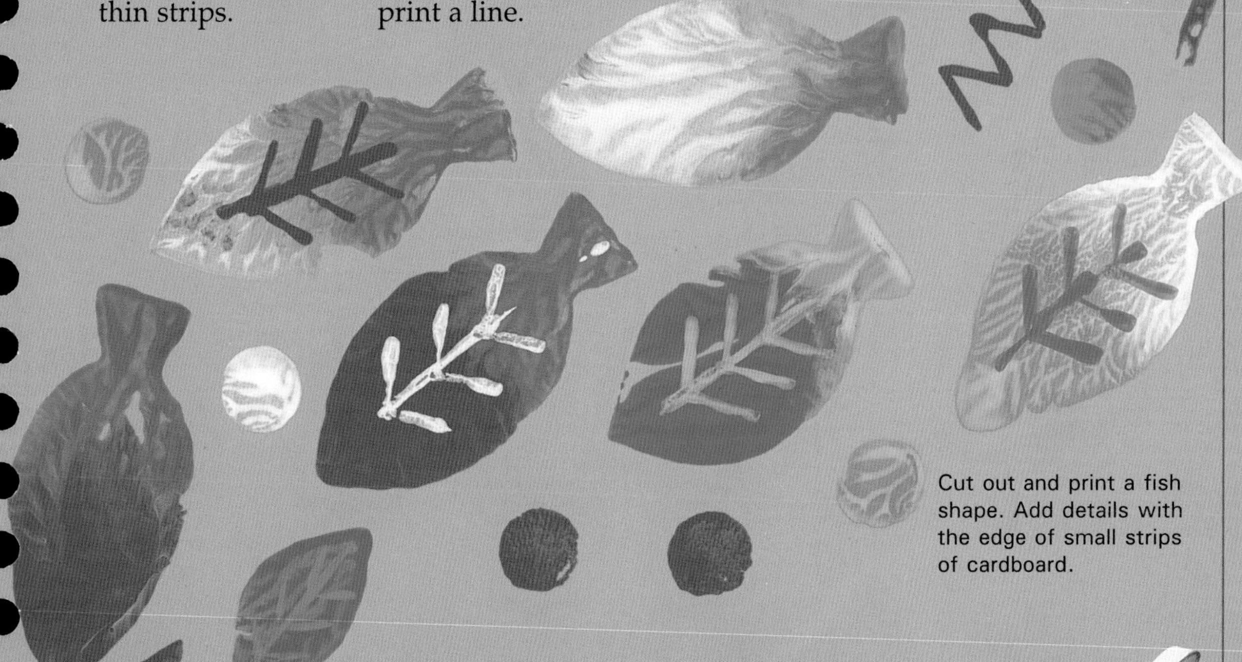

1. Cut different thicknesses of cardboard into thin strips.

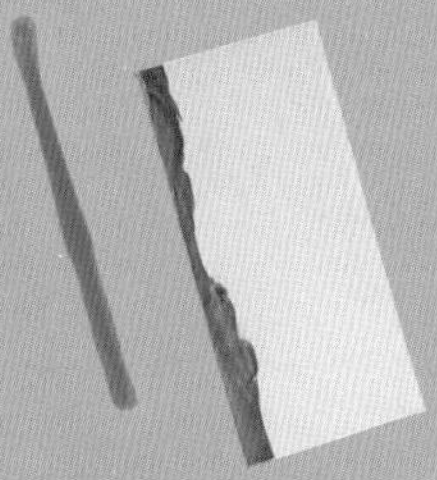

2. Dip the edge of the cardboard into the paint, then print a line.

The effect you get depends on the thickness of the cardboard.

Thin cardboard

Thick cardboard

Corrugated cardboard

Cut out and print a fish shape. Add details with the edge of small strips of cardboard.

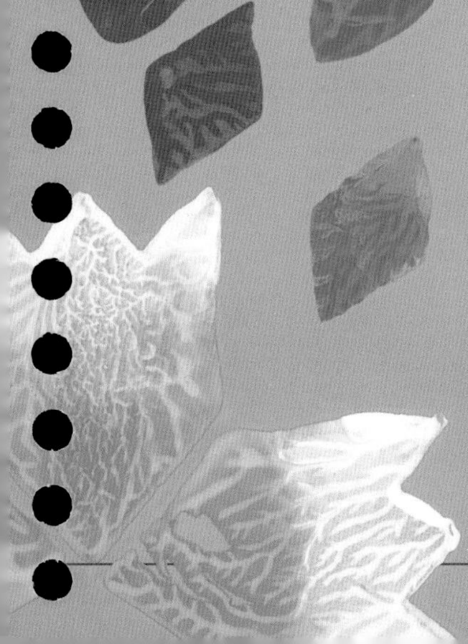

Curved shapes

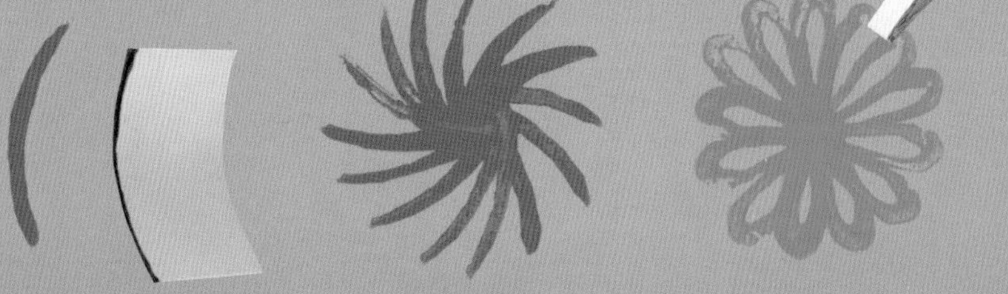

Dip the edge of a piece of cardboard into paint. Bend it as you print.

For a spiral, print curved shapes, joining them in the middle.

For a looped pattern, bend some thin cardboard and secure it with tape.

TURN OVER FOR MORE PRINTING IDEAS

More printed patterns

Twist this end.

Do several fan shapes to make a flower.

1. To make a fan shape, dip the edge of a piece of cardboard into some paint.

2. Twist the top of the cardboard as you print, keeping the bottom corner in one place.

Experiment with lots of different patterns and shapes.

Use the edge of cardboard for a stem. Print a small triangle for petals.

For a flower
like the one
above, overlap
three prints.

Dip a loop of cardboard
in two colors of paint
(see pages 18 and 19)
for a flower like this.

Ready-mix and poster paints

Ready-mix paints and poster paints are good for simple, bold pictures, although poster paints tend to give much brighter results than ready-mix paints. Both kinds of paint can be thinned with water.

Squeeze ready-mix paint onto a palette before you use it. Be careful if you mix these paints, as the colors can look dull when they dry. Poster paints can be used straight from the jar, or mix them with each other on a palette. The picture on the opposite page includes some colors that were mixed.

It's best to use thick bristol paper with these paints. Thinner paper will crinkle.

Poster paints are sold in little jars and are more expensive than ready-mix paints.

The picture below had outlines added with a felt-tip pen, once the paint was dry.

Rubber band prints

THICK CARDBOARD

1. Use a ballpoint pen to draw a simple design on a piece of thick cardboard.

2. Paint over the cardboard with a thick layer of household glue. Wash your brush.

3. Cut pieces of a thick rubber band to fit the main shapes. Press them on firmly.

4. Cut pieces of a narrower rubber band for the details. Press them onto the glue.

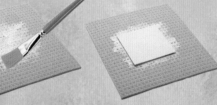

5. Cut squares from a thick rubber band. Press them onto the background.

6. When the glue has dried, paint some ready-mix paint onto a sponge cloth.

7. Put the cardboard, picture-side down, into the paint. Press on the back firmly.

8. Lay the painted cardboard on a pad of newspaper. Press all over the back, then lift it off.

9. Do several practice prints like this before doing a 'proper' print on paper.

Experiment by printing on different colors of paper.

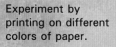

Prints on tissue paper

These prints work particularly well on bright tissue paper. Follow the steps below.

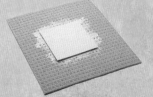

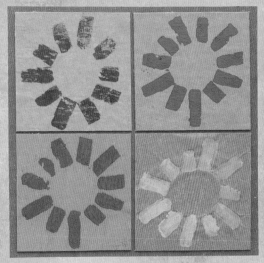

1. If you want to print on tissue paper, press the cardboard in some paint.

2. Carefully lay the painted cardboard, face-up, on a pile of newspaper.

Different colors printed on tissue paper

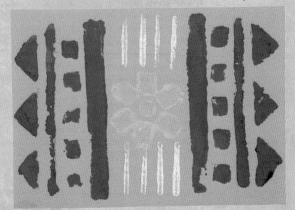

3. Lay a double layer of tissue paper on top and press gently. Peel it off carefully.

Use thick and thin rubber bands for a flower, like this.

For a multi-colored print, paint the rubber bands with different colors.

Gold acrylic paint on dark purple paper

Hand and cardboard prints

ANY LIGHT-COLORED PAPER

Turn over to page 28 to see a full-size version of the prints shown on these two pages.

You'll need to be near a sink and have lots of paper towels to wipe your hands.

1. For the background, brush some plastic foodwrap with blue paint.

2. Lay some paper on top of it and press lightly. Lift off the paper and leave it to dry.

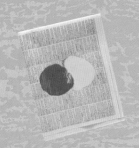

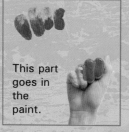

This part goes in the paint.

This part goes in the paint.

3. For a seahorse, pour two shades of ready-mix or poster paint onto a pad of newspapers.

4. For the head, press the top of your fingers into the paint. Print them on the paper.

5. Press your knuckles into the paint. Turn your hand sideways and print a body.

6. Put paint on your little finger as far as your knuckle. Print a long snout with it.

Fins

This is the start of the tail.

Do smaller and smaller prints.

7. Use the same finger to print three fins and three more prints below the body.

8. Use a fingertip to add two prints at the end of the snout. Print some along the head.

9. Finish the tail by doing several prints with a fingertip. Curve them around.

10. Dip a fingertip in a bright color and print an eye. Add the middle when it's dry.

Crabs

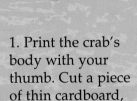 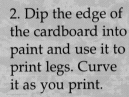  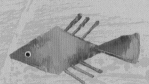

1. Print the crab's body with your thumb. Cut a piece of thin cardboard, about 1in. long.

2. Dip the edge of the cardboard into paint and use it to print legs. Curve it as you print.

3. Use a small piece of cardboard to print V-shaped pincers on the front legs.

4. Print stalks for eyes. Do the eyes with a fingertip. Add dots when the paint is dry.

Fan fish

1. Dip the edge of a piece of thin cardboard into two or three colors of paint.

2. Press it onto your paper, then twist one end to make a fan shape. Turn the paper.

3. Print another fan to finish the body. Then print a narrower one for the tail.

4. Print the fins with cardboard. Do the eye with a fingertip when the paint is dry.

Little rainbow fish

  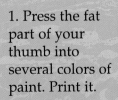  

1. Press the fat part of your thumb into several colors of paint. Print it.

2. Add a tail with a fingertip. For the eye, dip the end of an old pencil in paint, then print it.

27

READYMIX AND POSTER PAINTS

The instructions for these prints are on pages 26-27.

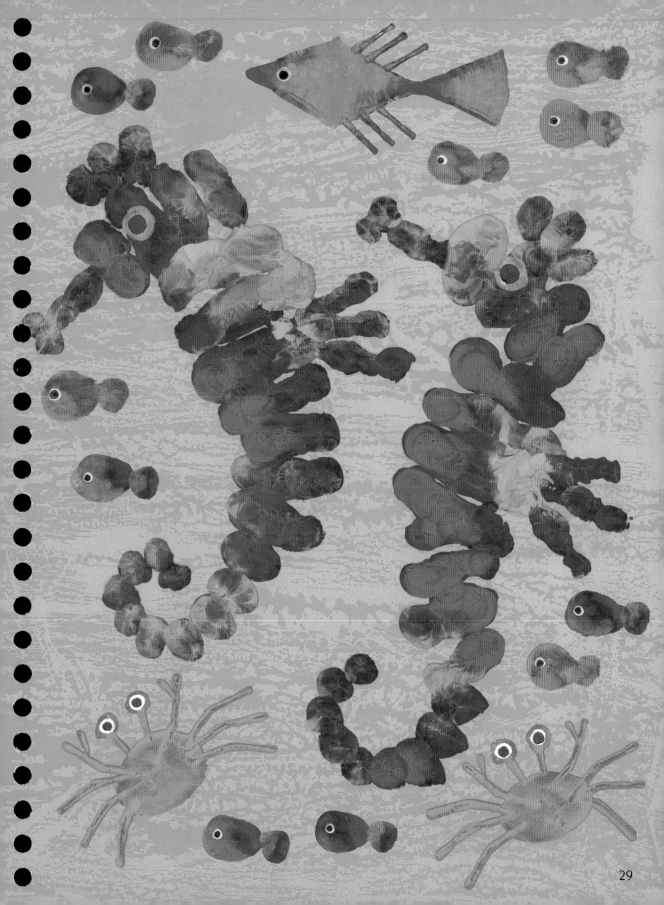

29

Masking out and splattering

A COLORED PIECE OF PAPER AND ANOTHER PIECE THE SAME SIZE.

1. Put the colored paper to one side. Draw an outline on the other piece. Cut it out.

2. Lay newspapers outside. Put small stones around the edge to weight them down.

3. Put the colored paper on the newspapers, with the cut-out on top. Weight it down.

4. Pour some ready-mix paint into a container. Add water to make it runny.

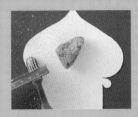   

5. Dip a toothbrush into the paint. Pull a ruler along the bristles <u>toward</u> you to splatter the paint.

6. Continue splattering paint around the cut-out until the speckles are very dense.

7. Lift the paper cut-out to leave the area you masked out. Leave it to dry.

8. Add details and shading such as windows and a watery reflection, with pastels.

Pulled cardboard prints

USE THICK CARDBOARD

1. Put some paint on a plate. Dip the edge of a piece of cardboard into it.

2. Put the painted edge onto your paper and pull it evenly to the side.

3. Dip the edge in the paint again, then pull it toward you.

4. For a diamond shape, pull the board diagonally out to one side.

Use a different piece of cardboard for each color you use.

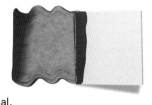

Keep the edge vertical.

5. For a zigzag effect pull the edge diagonally down, then up.

6. For a wiggly line, pull the edge to one side in a wavy motion.

Print a tree with several overlapping curves.

Zigzag roofs

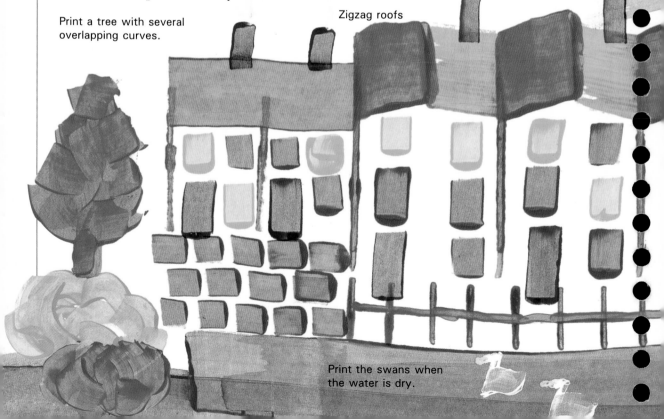

Print the swans when the water is dry.

Swans and ducks

Bricks

Start here.

1. Dip the edge of a piece of cardboard in paint and print a line.

2. Move the edge below the line and pull the edge in a wavy line.

3. Use the edge of a piece of cardboard for the head and beak.

Print in rows with narrow cardboard in a darker shade of paint.

For hills, do long wavy prints with a wide piece of cardboard. Make them overlap.

Paint and tissue paper

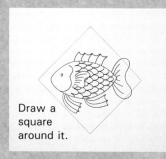

Draw a square around it.

Use your picture as a guide.

1. Use a thick black felt-tip pen to draw a bold drawing of a fish. Do it on white paper.

2. Trace the main shapes of your fish onto different colors of tissue paper, then cut them out.

3. Cut a piece of polythene from a clear plastic bag. Make sure it's bigger than your drawing.

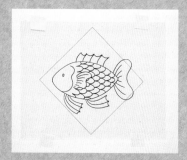

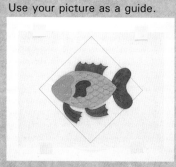

4. Lay the polythene over your drawing. Put pieces of tape along the edges to secure it.

5. Brush the tissue paper shapes with household glue. Press each one in place onto the polythene.

6. Cut or tear strips of tissue paper for the background. Glue them on around the fish.

7. Glue a piece of pale blue tissue paper over the whole picture, then leave to it dry.

8. When the glue is completely dry, carefully peel the tissue paper off the polythene.

9. Place the tissue paper over your drawing. Go over your outlines using black paint.

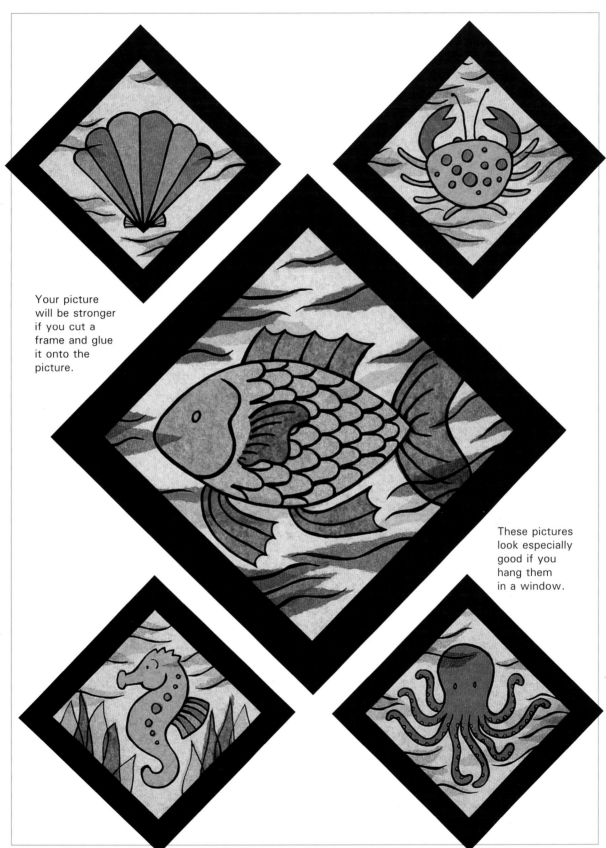

Your picture will be stronger if you cut a frame and glue it onto the picture.

These pictures look especially good if you hang them in a window.

35

About colors

Which colors go well together? Why do some colors appear to jump out of a painting and some seem to blend in with the colors around them? These pages show how different combinations of colors alter the way a painting looks.

Primary colors

There are three colors that cannot be made by mixing other colors. These are red, yellow and blue, and they are known as primary colors.

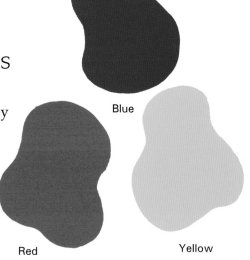

Blue

Red

Yellow

Secondary colors

If you mix each of the primary colors with another one, you get orange, green and purple. These are known as secondary colors.

Red + yellow

Yellow + blue

Blue + red

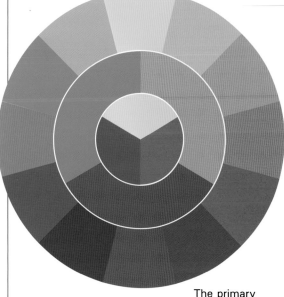

The secondary colors are in the middle ring of the color circle.

The primary colors are in the center of the color circle.

More colors

You can get more colors by mixing a primary with a secondary color. These mixes are shown on the outside ring of the color circle.

If you mix yellow with orange you get a color between the two.

Blue mixed with green makes a bluey-green.

Red and orange make an orangey-red.

Harmonic colors

Harmonic colors are those which lie near each other on the outside ring of the color circle, such as blue, light blue, green and light green.

These are examples of different groups of harmonic colors.

Complementary colors

The colors that lie diagonally opposite each other in the color circle are called complementary colors. They have the most contrast when they are painted next to each other.

When you paint complementary colors next to each other they 'buzz' and make your eyes bounce.

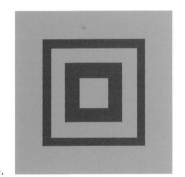
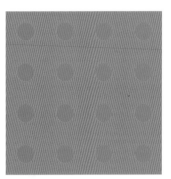

Warm and cool colors

Some colors give the feeling of warmth or coldness and are actually known as warm or cool colors. Warm colors look brighter and stand out more in a picture than cool colors.

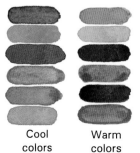

Cool colors   Warm colors

The cool colors used in this picture give it a cold, icy feeling.

Color and tone

The tone of a color is how light or dark it is. You can create unusual pictures by painting in tones of one color or by changing the tones in a picture.

This circle shows the tones of different colors.

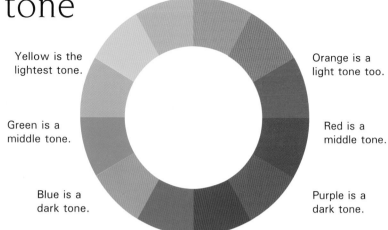

Yellow is the lightest tone.

Orange is a light tone too.

Green is a middle tone.

Red is a middle tone.

Blue is a dark tone.

Purple is a dark tone.

Experimenting with tones

Experiment with making as many different tones of one color as you can. Always start with the lightest tone and get gradually darker. This is easiest to do with acrylic, poster or ready-mix paints.

All these tones were made by adding a color to white.

Start with white. Add a tiny amount of a color.

Add more and more of the color until you get a dark tone.

Light and dark tones

The tones in a picture can change the feeling or mood of it. Light tones give a soft, pastel effect, whereas dark tones make a picture look stronger.

Compare the picture at the top, which is painted using light tones only, with the one at the bottom, which is painted in darker tones.

Similar tones

Although colors look very different they can have the same tones. It's easiest to see the similarities between colors in a black and white picture.

Compare the tones in the color, and the black and white photographs. For instance, the red paper and blue squares have a similar tone.

The flowers have the lightest tone. The purple squares on the paper have the darkest tone.

In this black and white photograph it's easier to see which colors have a similar tone.

Reversing tones

You can get some surprising effects if you reverse the order of tones, so that yellow becomes the darkest tone and blue becomes the lightest one.

The tones in the second picture below have been reversed. Any part of the picture that was a dark color has become lighter.

Light blue has become dark blue.

Inks

Inks are ideal for painting or drawing bright, vibrant pictures. Use them with a brush, a dip pen or draw with a cartridge pen. They are also ideal for resist techniques with wax crayons (see page 76) or oil pastels.

Use straight from a bottle or cartridge pen or mix them with water.

Undiluted ink

Watered-down ink.

Paint ink over oil pastels or wax crayons for a resist effect.

Ink blobs

Wet a piece of watercolor paper then drop spots of ink on it. When the paper is dry, draw on top with a felt-tip or dip pen.

Try doing blobs close together. Let the colors bleed into each other.

Stripes

The colors change where they overlap.

1. On dry paper, paint stripes of different colors. Vary the thickness.

2. When the ink is dry, brush stripes across the other stripes.

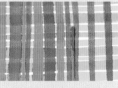

Spooky trees

1. Paint a wash with watercolor paints (see page 48). Leave it to dry.

2. Paint a line of black ink. Use a straw to blow the ink into shapes.

Scratched resist

1. Use a pencil to draw a random pattern all over a piece of paper.

2. Draw a line next to the ones already drawn to make double lines.

3. Fill in the shapes using oil pastels. Try not to go over the lines.

4. Brush black drawing ink all over the paper. Leave it to dry.

Use the corner of a screwdriver to scrape the patterns.

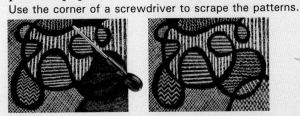

5. Scrape a pattern through the ink to reveal the color underneath.

6. Continue scraping different patterns into all the shapes.

Warning!

Ink will stain your clothes, so always wear something to protect you when you use them. Don't forget to rinse your brush or dip pen, too.

Brush and ink paintings

ANY THICK WHITE PAPER

The best kind of brush to use for pictures like these, are soft-haired brushes that have a pointed tip. Chinese or Japanese lettering brushes are ideal for these techniques.

Use a soft brush with a pointed tip.

Mixing the inks

To do the paintings on these pages, you need to use three shades of one color of ink. Use ink from a bottle.

Add a few drops of ink to water in a small container to make a watery ink.

Mix a medium shade, by adding more drops of ink to water in another container.

Undiluted ink. Use straight from a bottle.

Bamboo

Practice on scrap paper before doing a large picture.

Use the width of the bristles to paint.

Don't put more ink on your brush.

Use the tip of the brush to begin with, then increase the pressure.

1. Dip your brush in the watery ink, then dab the bristles on a paper towel. Paint a section of a stem.

2. Paint another two sections above the first one. Leave a small space between each section.

3. Using the medium ink and the tip of your brush, add branches coming out from the stem.

Use undiluted ink.

Press lightly.

4. Add twigs onto the branches. Leave a small space between one twig and the next one.

5. For a leaf, press lightly on the tip of the brush, then press a little harder. Then press lightly again.

6. Use the tip of the brush and undiluted ink to paint grass and lines at the joints on the stem.

Bird

For each line, start with the tip, then press harder, then lighter again.

1. Using undiluted ink, paint the beak with the tip of your brush. Add the neck and body.

2. Paint the head, an eye and a line for the bird's back. Add a branch at the bottom of the body.

Make the lines different lengths.

3. For a tail, paint several joining lines onto the body.

43

Brush paintings
WATERCOLOR OR BRISTOL PAPER

All the pictures on these pages were painted using three shades of ink. You paint the main shapes, then details are added with a very fine brush or dip pen. Before you begin, follow the steps on page 42 for mixing the ink.

Bugs

1. Use the medium ink to paint a body. Add wings with the watery ink.

2. Add a head, eyes, antennae and legs with undiluted ink.

Fish

1. Use the very watery ink to paint a simple shape of a fish.

2. Add the head, gills and underside of the fish with the medium ink.

3. Use a pen or fine brush and undiluted ink to add an outline.

4. Add an eye, mouth, fins and a tail with the undiluted ink.

Paint a lily pad with different shades of ink.

For a background like this, paint a watercolor wash (see page 48). Let it dry before adding the creatures.

Use the tip of a thin brush to paint reeds.

Frog

1. Use the very watery ink to paint a shape for the body.

2. Use the tip of the brush to add a darker stripe along the shape with the medium ink.

3. Before the body has dried, add some spots of the medium ink to it.

4. Use undiluted ink to draw an eye. Outline the body and add a leg.

45

Watercolor paints

Watercolor paints can give you bright, vibrant colors, but they are also particularly good for painting skies and water.

Paints

Most watercolor paints are sold in tubes or as small, solid blocks, called pans or trays. The pans are easy to use and are more economical.

The paint in tubes is quite thick. Mix it with water on a palette.

Boxes of watercolors are filled with pans. You can buy each color separately.

Watercolor paper

Watercolor paper comes in different thicknesses and with different textures. You can buy it from art shops in blocks, spiral-bound pads and as individual sheets.

The thickness of the paper is shown by its weight. Look for paper which is 90lb or above. It won't wrinkle very much when you paint on it.

The paper in watercolor blocks is glued around the edges. Slip a blunt knife into the gap. Gently cut the piece of paper away from the block.

Rough watercolor paper has the most texture.

Hot-pressed or Smooth paper has the smoothest surface.

'Not' or cold-pressed paper has a semi-rough texture.

A block of watercolor paper

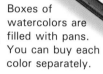

Most of the watercolor projects in this book were done on 'not' paper.

Mixing watercolors

If you have tubes of watercolor paints, mix them in the same way as you would mix acrylics. Find out how to do this on page 10. These steps show you how to mix paint from pans.

1. Dip your brush in water, then blot it on a paper towel to get rid of some of the water.

2. Move the brush around and around in one color until the bristles are covered in paint.

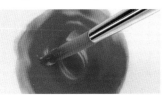

3. Dab the paint onto a palette, then repeat the steps to make a larger patch of color.

4. Rinse and blot your brush on a paper towel, then dip it into the color you want to mix in.

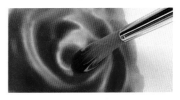

5. Mix this paint with the first color on the palette. Repeat until you get the color you want.

Watercolor paints look darker when they are wet. They become lighter once they are dry.

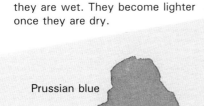

Prussian blue

All these colors were made by mixing Prussian blue and carmine.

If you want to mix a lot of one color, put a little water into a container and mix the paint into it.

Carmine

47

Experimenting with watercolors

WATERCOLOR PAPER

Watercolors can be used in lots of different ways. Experiment with these techniques on pieces of scrap watercolor paper.

Painting a wash

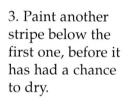

Overlap the stripes slightly.

1. Mix up plenty of paint in a container. You need enough to cover your paper.

2. Use a thick brush to paint a broad stripe across the top of the paper.

3. Paint another stripe below the first one, before it has had a chance to dry.

4. Continue adding more stripes down the paper until it is covered.

Lifting off paint

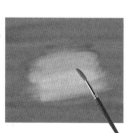

Before the paint dries in your wash, use a cotton swab to lift off some paint.

Lift off some of the paint with a scrunched up tissue. This gives a different effect.

You can also lift off paint with a clean brush. Dry it on a paper towel first.

Try using a clean sponge too. If you dab it on the paint, you get a textured effect.

Wet paper effects

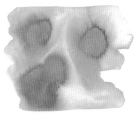 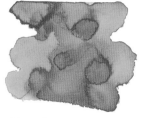 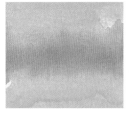 

Wet a piece of paper with a sponge or thick brush. Paint small blobs on it.

Try the same thing but use two colors. The colors will bleed into each other.

Paint a wash in one color. Before it dries, paint a stripe in a different color.

Paint a wash. Drop blobs of clean water onto the paint and let it spread.

Color blends

1. Wipe a clean, wet sponge across your paper to make it wet.

2. Mix two different colors of watercolors on a palette.

3. Cover about a third of the paper with a wash in one color.

4. Turn the paper upside down and paint on a second wash of color.

5. Brush across the paper to blend the colors where they meet.

Try blending three colors together.

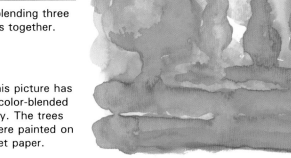

This picture has a color-blended sky. The trees were painted on wet paper.

Painting on wet paper

WATERCOLOR PAPER

Before you do the project on these pages, try out this technique on some spare scrap paper.

1. Put three colors of watercolor paint on a palette.

2. Use a sponge or a big clean brush to paint water all over the paper.

The paint will spread.

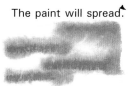

3. Brush short, light strokes of color onto the wet paper.

Experiment with different combinations of colors.

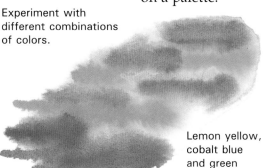

Lemon yellow, cobalt blue and green

Let the second color run into the first one.

4. Wet another piece of paper. Use two different colors of paint.

5. Try another sample with three colors of paint. Let the colors run.

Windmills and a canal

1. Mix patches of two different blues and green watercolor paint.

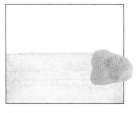

2. Use a sponge or a clean brush to wet the bottom half of the paper.

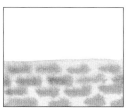

3. Brush short, strokes of one of the blues, all over the wet area.

4. Add strokes of the other blue and green. Let them run into each other.

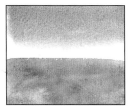

5. Wet the paper at the top. Paint a pale blue wash for the sky.

6. When the paint has dried, paint a green stripe and windmill shapes.

7. Use the tip of a thin brush to add lines for the windmills' sails.

8. Use green to paint the leaves in the foreground. Add red tulips.

The sea in these pictures was painted first, then the sky was added. Details were added with watercolors once the background had dried.

Water painting

WATERCOLOR OR THICK BRISTOL PAPER

This is another idea which shows how watercolor paints spread on wet paper.

Before you start, mix a tiny amount of blue paint with a little water to make a very watery paint.

The paint spreads up to the outline.

1. Paint the outline of a simple shape with the watery paint. Fill in the shape with water.

2. Mix some other colors. While the shape is still wet, paint a blob of color inside it.

3. Add other blobs of color so that they run together. Leave it flat to dry.

Paint the trunk of the tree first, then the leaves.

Paint the butterfly's feelers with a thin brush.

Use greens and blues for the lower leaves. Paint red, yellow and orange leaves near the top.

53

Blow paintings

ANY KIND OF THICK PAPER

The colors will mix.

1. Mix two colors of paint with water. Make them runny.

2. Pour some of each color onto paper, close together.

3. Place a straw above the middle of the paint and blow very hard.

4. As you blow, 'chase' the paint outward to make spiky shapes.

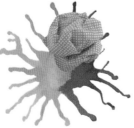

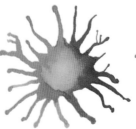

5. Keep on blowing the paint out in different directions.

6. Gently blot the middle of the paint with the corner of a damp rag.

7. Then, go around and around wiping the paint into the shape of a face.

8. Leave to dry. Then, paint eyes on the face with a fine brush.

9. Paint eyebrows and a nose. Add thin lips and spiky ears.

Use harmonic colors, such as blue and green, red and orange or red and purple.

Painting skies

WATERCOLOR PAPER

Watercolors are very good for painting skies and clouds. Use different shades of blue to suggest different types of skies. You can find lots more different techniques for painting skies on pages 130-133.

Cloudy sky

1. Wet the paper with a sponge or brush. Paint a wash of cobalt blue.

2. For fluffy clouds, use the corner of a tissue to dab off patches of paint.

Different types of sky

Paint a wash with two shades of blue for a 'heavy' sky.

Paint a yellow and orange wash.

Add the trees when the wash has dried.

For rain clouds, dab off paint, then add a darker line along the bottom of each cloud.

Paint a purple wash, then dab off color with a tissue and a brush.

A stormy sky

These steps show you how to paint a dark, stormy sky.

You will need Prussian blue, burnt umber and yellow ocher watercolors for this picture.

1. Use a thick brush or clean sponge to wet the paper all over.

2. Mix Prussian blue with burnt umber to make dark gray.

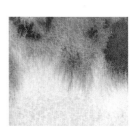

3. Blob the gray paint in patches onto the top part of the paper.

4. Add some patches of yellow ocher with the tip of your brush.

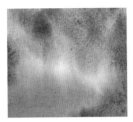

5. Mix different shades of green (see page 9). Add them at the bottom.

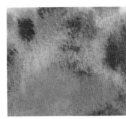

6. Continue to add more greens. Let them bleed into the gray sky.

7. Let the sky dry a little, then paint a castle, using the gray from step 2.

Salt paintings

WATERCOLOR PAPER

If you sprinkle salt onto watercolor paint, the salt soaks up the color, and leaves a grainy effect when it dries.

Paint quickly, as the paint has to be wet when you sprinkle on the salt.

1. Paint a whale, then paint stripes for the sea, leaving a space between the stripes.

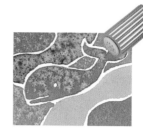

2. Before the paint has dried, sprinkle lots of salt all over the paper.

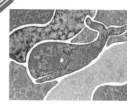

3. As the paint dries, it soaks up the salt. Leave the paint and salt to dry.

4. Shake off any excess salt, then either rub off all the salt or leave some of it on.

Paint things around the whale. Keep their shapes simple.

The salt has been left on this painting, giving the background a sandy, textured effect.

Adding highlights

Highlights make pictures come to life. They can also make things look shiny, as if they are made of glass or metal. Here are two ways of adding highlights. If you are painting with watercolors, always do the highlights by leaving a space.

Adding highlights make things such as this bird's eye, look shiny.

Paper highlights

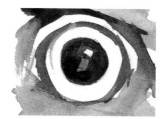

1. Draw two circles. Fill in the inner one, leaving a small diamond-shaped space. Paint around the outside of the larger circle.

2. Use darker paint to outline the eye. Go over the inner circle, leaving another space beside the first one.

3. Fill the eye with orange paint. Add blue-gray lines below the eye to give the eye socket some shape.

Adding white

1. Draw a robot's body. Paint over your drawing with black paint.

2. Add some white paint to the black. Paint lines inside all the shapes.

3. Mix in some more white paint. Fill in the parts shown here.

4. Wash your brush well, then add white lines inside each shape.

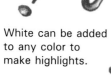
White can be added to any color to make highlights.

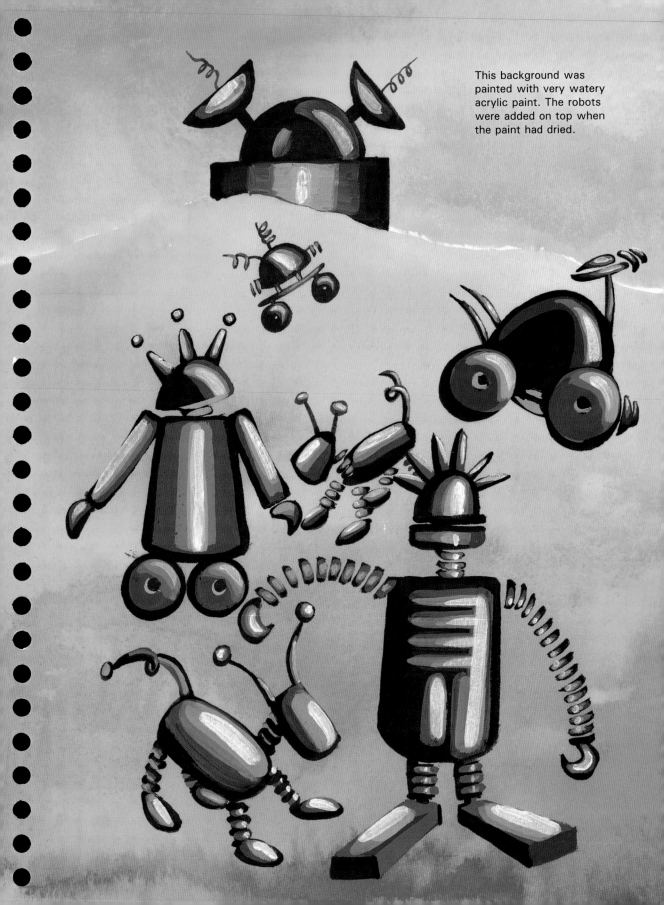

This background was painted with very watery acrylic paint. The robots were added on top when the paint had dried.

Painting perspective

ANY KIND OF PAPER

Painting pictures in perspective means doing them the way your eye sees them. Colors appear to fade the further away they are. Use any kind of paint and thick paper for painting the pictures on these pages.

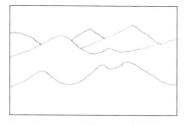

1. Draw outlines of hills in pencil. Start with the one closest to you.

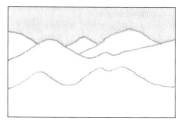

2. Mix a little blue and a spot of red with some water. Fill in the sky.

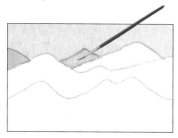

3. Add a little more blue to the paint. Fill in the furthest hills.

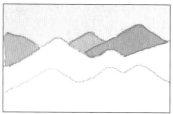

4. Add more blue and red to make the paint darker. Fill in the next hill.

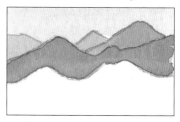

5. Continue adding more blue and red paint until all the hills are filled in.

This picture was painted in watercolors on watercolor paper.

This picture was created by painting the houses, sea, curtain and hills first. The window frame and cat were painted once the rest were dry.

Chalk pastels

Chalk pastels, or soft pastels, are very soft and they smudge easily. This means that you can get some great effects by mixing and blending them.

Hold a pastel like a pencil and use the end to draw marks like the zigzags, above.

Lay the pastel flat on the paper.

You can also draw with the side of a pastel. Snap it in half and peel off any paper.

Mixing colors

You can mix pastels on your paper by doing strokes one on top of the other.

Experiment with the order in which you use the pastels. Do you get different colors?

Blending

1. You can also blend pastels. Draw overlapping strokes in different colors.

2. Then, smudge the colors together with a finger. This gives a soft effect.

If you don't want to get your fingers messy, then use a cotton swab instead.

Graduating colors

The colors mix in the middle.

1. Starting at the top, use the side of a pastel to do strokes across your paper.

2. Do more strokes, with another pastel. Overlap some of the first color.

Broken colors

1. Start in the middle. Draw lots of short strokes in one color around a central point.

2. Fill in some of the spaces with other short strokes in different colors.

Dotted pictures

   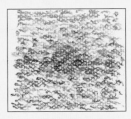

1. Use the end of orange and red pastels to draw short strokes for a sun.

2. Draw a line of light blue and dark blue strokes across the middle of the sun.

3. Draw yellow and orange strokes around the sun. Add some in the sky.

4. Use different shades of blue for the sky and the sea. Add pink strokes too.

Paper for pastels

You can get some good effects with pastels if you draw on colored paper. For the best results, use paper which has a slightly rough or textured surface.

Art stores sell colored paper for pastels.

Pastels work very well on black paper.

Construction paper is good and it's also cheap.

A pastel fantasy landscape

BRISTOL PAPER

1. Draw two curved bands, using a black chalk pastel.

2. Fill in the space between the bands with a dark blue pastel.

3. Add a band of yellow, then another band of dark blue.

4. Fill in with diagonal strokes of black and ultramarine blue.

5. Do long white strokes on top of the bands of black, to make gray.

6. Blend all the colors with your finger or a cotton swab (see page 64).

7. Wash your hands or use several cotton swabs. They will get dirty.

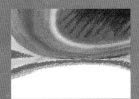

8. Draw a gray line across your paper. Add red and yellow stripes above it.

9. Draw different sizes of circles and lots of wavy lines in the foreground.

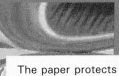
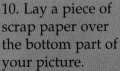

The paper protects your picture.

10. Lay a piece of scrap paper over the bottom part of your picture.

11. Draw moons and stars in the sky. Then gently blend them in.

12. Draw clouds on the horizon with gray or a mixture of black and white.

13. Use yellow to add a wavy highlight along each cloud.

14. Blend the foreground, but leave the clouds as they are.

More chalk techniques

These pages show you two more techniques for mixing colors with chalk pastels. In both techniques, you don't rub the colors to blend them; the colors mix where they overlap.

Experiment with different shapes, patterns and colors.

Remember the color of the paper you draw on affects the colors the pastels make.

Blocking

Use the side of a chalk pastel to fill in areas of color. This is known as blocking. Then go over the top with another color of pastel.

Hatching

Use the end of a pastel to build up layers of short diagonal lines. Try using different combinations of colors.

Draw the lines in the same direction.

Try hatching on top of a block of color.

Landscape

1. Use the side of a turquoise chalk pastel to block in the sky. Leave gaps for the trees.

2. Add patches of pale blue to the sky, then some dark blue over the top.

3. Use the side of red, yellow and orange pastels to fill in the shape of the trees.

4. Add hatching on top of each tree with different colors. Let them merge together.

5. Use the side of green, yellow and orange pastels to add stripes below the sky.

6. Add hatching on top of the stripes. Make them get longer in the foreground.

7. Use the end of a black pastel to draw a line below the trees. Add branches, too.

Oil pastels

Oil pastels give you very bright, strong colors. They don't smudge in the way chalk pastels do. This makes them easier to use. You can do lots of the same things with oil pastels that you can do with chalk pastels.

Like chalk pastels, oil pastels work well on colored paper which has a slightly textured surface.

Try doing short strokes in the same direction in different colors.

Use them on their side to fill in areas of color. Peel off the paper and break them in half, first.

Try doing lots of overlapping strokes in different colors.

You can draw on black paper with oil pastels, although the colors you get may change slightly.

A white oil pastel shows up well on brightly colored paper.

Mixing colors

To mix colors, use one color on top of another (see the tiger opposite). The colors blend together.

Oil pastels work well on bristol paper, construction paper or newsprint paper.

A tiger in long grass

1. Draw a straight purple line about a third of the way down the paper.

2. Add hills above the line. Fill in the sky with pale blue and white.

3. Fill in parts of the hills with gray, to make them look far away.

4. Use the side of an orange pastel to fill in the foreground.

5. Draw the outline of a tiger on top of the foreground.

6. Add patterns on the fur with orange, yellow and black.

7. Let the black stripes blend with the other colors where they overlap.

8. Draw lots of long grass in front of the tiger with greens and brown.

71

Color and patterns

Oil pastels give you strong, vibrant colors. Use them to experiment with colors. Try putting different colors together and see how one color affects another.

The blue square in the yellow square looks brighter than the same blue in the gray.

The green in the red square appears to be stronger than the same green in the gray square.

Experimenting with colors

Try putting different warm colors together.

Try cool colors, such as greens and blues.

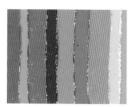

Try warm and cool colors, in thick and thin stripes.

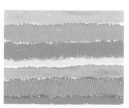

Experiment with bright and pale colors together.

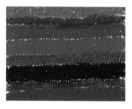

Try dark colors, such as blue, purple and brown.

Do alternate stripes of dark and light colors.

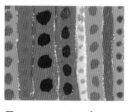

Draw spots along the stripes. Make them different sizes.

Draw thin lines or zigzags along some stripes.

A card idea

1. Draw a large box with a purple pastel. Draw an orange box inside.

2. Draw yellow triangles. Fill in between them with green.

3. Outline the triangles with a darker green. Add red dots.

4. Draw a red fence. Add a purple line down one side.

5. Draw the hen's body and color it in. Leave a blank circle for the eye.

6. Add the beak, plumage, tail and feet. Fill them in and add stripes to the feet.

7. Fill in the sky. Add some shading with darker blue and purple around the edges.

8. Add some black lines to the hen's body. Outline the eye and add a pupil.

Oil pastel effects

ANY WHITE PAPER

Stained glass effect

Draw the outline in pencil first if you want to.

Press hard.

1. Fold your paper in half, then open it out. Draw half a butterfly with a black oil pastel.

2. Fold the paper in half again, then rub all over one side with the handle of a pair of scissors.

3. Unfold the paper. Use the pastel to draw over the faint outline of the other half of the butterfly.

4. Draw leaves in the background. Paint inks in the sections between all the outlines.

Ink outlines

Leave a gap between each section.

 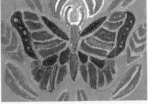 

1. Follow steps 1-3 on page 74, but use a pencil to draw the outline. Fill in the spaces between the outline with oil pastels.

2. Paint all over your picture with a bright color of ink. It will fill the gaps between the colored sections.

3. Use the edge of a screwdriver to scratch details on the butterfly's wings and on the leaves in the background.

Wax crayons

Wax crayons can be used in lots of different ways. You can get lots of shades with one crayon by varying the amount of pressure you use. You can also mix them to make different colors. They are also good for doing rubbings and resist effects.

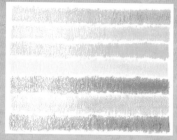

This shows some different shades you can get when you vary the pressure as you draw.

You can also mix wax crayons, although they don't blend together as well as chalk or oil pastels.

Wax resist stars

Press hard.

1. Draw stars all over your paper. Use two colors for each star. Add a trail from each star.

2. Mix up lots of dark blue watercolor paint in a container. Don't make it too thin and watery.

3. Brush the paint across the paper, covering your drawing. The crayon resists the paint.

Fantasy bird

1. Draw a large bird with a pencil. Press lightly to get a faint outline.

Look at the big picture to see the white lines to draw.

2. Draw feathers on the head, body and tail with a white wax crayon. Draw lines on the feet, too.

3. Mix up some orange paint in a container. Paint all over the picture.

4. Use a fine brush to paint details on the body and head. Use dark red paint.

5. Add more details to the feathers using the dark red paint.

6. Paint around the eye, beak and feet. Add stripes to them.

Wax resist rubbings

THIN WHITE PAPER

 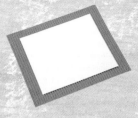  

1. Snap a wax crayon in half. Then, peel off any protective paper around it.

2. Lay a piece of thin paper on a textured surface, such as corrugated cardboard.

3. Rub the side of the crayon over the paper so that a pattern of the texture appears.

4. Paint over your rubbing with a contrasting color of watercolor paint or ink.

5. Do more rubbings on different surfaces. Paint the rubbings in different colors.

6. On another piece of paper, draw a street of houses. Make each one different.

7. Cut the rubbings into strips. Glue on three or four pieces to make one house.

8. Add windows, doors, roof tiles and brickwork on top with a black wax crayon.

More resist effects

ANY THICK PAPER

1. Using bright wax crayons, draw a patterned stripe near the bottom of the paper.

2. Use different crayons to draw buildings. Add lots of domes, towers and windows.

3. Add some trees. Use bright crayons to color in the walls and roofs of the buildings.

4. Paint all over the picture with a dark shade of ready-mix or poster paint.

5. Dab a damp, crumpled cloth over the waxy parts to lift off some of the paint.

6. Leave it to dry. Then, scratch patterns and shading into the crayon with a toothpick.

Cracked wax effect

THIN PAPER, SUCH AS TYPING PAPER

This is a different resist technique using wax crayons. It works best if your picture covers the paper.

Cracks appear in the crayoned parts when you crumple up the paper (see step 3). These allow the paint to seep through, leaving a cracked effect.

1. Draw a flower in a pot with wax crayons. Color them in, pressing hard.

2. Fill in the background with crayon. Press hard and leave no gaps.

3. Crumple the paper in from the corners. Be careful not to tear it.

4. Open out the paper. Crumple it again, so that you get lots of cracks.

5. Flatten your picture. Paint all over with dark poster paint or ready-mix.

6. Make sure that you have brushed paint into all the cracks.

7. Rinse both sides under running water. Let the water drip off. Let it dry.

Use a warm setting on your iron.

8. If your picture is crinkly, iron it between two pieces of newspaper.

Creating textured papers

Many of the pages in this book have coloured backgrounds. These pages tell you how some of them were created and also gives you other ideas. Also look on pages 126-127 and 212-215 for more techniques.

This paper was created by dropping blobs of ink onto wet watercolor paper.

This rubbing was done with yellow wax crayon on the large holes of a cheese grater. The rubbing was then painted with ink.

This rubbing was done on the small holes on a cheese grater. See pages 78-79 for more rubbings.

For this effect, sprinkle salt onto wet watercolor paint. Let it dry, then rub off all the salt. See page 58 for a picture using this technique.

Paint a piece of plastic foodwrap with paint. Lay a piece of paper on top. Rub lightly over the paper, then lift it off (see pages 24 and 26).

This background was also done with paint on plastic foodwrap (see below left).

These pieces were painted with a household paintbrush. Paint on one color, then brush another color on top when dry. See pages 90-91 for a background like this.

This paper was painted with watercolor paints. It was then splattered with clean water while the paint was wet. Step 6 on page 31 shows you how to splatter.

Rub the side of a wax crayon over a piece of paper then paint it all over (see the background on page 82).

Splattered paper collage

COLORED PAPER, SUCH AS CONSTRUCTION PAPER

Weight the newspaper with small stones.

1. This can be very messy so do this outside. Put your paper onto some newspapers.

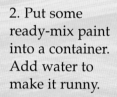    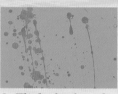

2. Put some ready-mix paint into a container. Add water to make it runny.

3. Dip an old toothbrush into the paint. Then, hold the brush over the paper.

4. Pull a ruler along the brush toward you, so the paint splatters onto the paper.

5. Keep splattering more paint on top until you get the effect you want. Let it dry.

6. Mix another color of paint and splatter it in the same way on top of the first one.

7. To get big splatters, dip a household paintbrush into runny paint.

8. Flick the brush sharply downward over the paper. Repeat with more paint.

9. Continue flicking the paint until you have the pattern you want. Leave it to dry.

10. Draw the outline of a frog and leaves on the back of the big splattered paper.

11. Draw some cattails and a strip for water on the finely splattered paper.

12. Cut out the shapes and glue them onto a piece of contrasting paper.

Tissue paper painting

ANY THICK PAPER

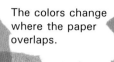

The colors change where the paper overlaps.

1. Rip some shapes from different colors of tissue paper.

2. Put some household glue into a container. Mix in a few drops of water.

3. Glue the tissue shapes onto white paper. Overlap some pieces.

4. Add more paper. The colors get stronger as you build up the layers.

Draw on top of the tissue paper. You don't need to outline the paper exactly.

Add dots and lines to the leaves.

Poppies

1. Tear red and orange tissue paper into large petal shapes.

2. Glue one petal. Press it onto a large piece of white paper.

3. Add three more petals. Overlap and crumple the paper in places.

4. Cut leaves and stems from tissue paper. Glue them around the poppies.

5. Brush glue over the poppies. This makes them slightly shiny.

6. When the glue is completely dry, use a thin felt-tip pen to add details.

Making cards and frames

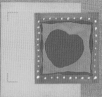

1. Fold some thin cardboard in half. Run a fingernail along the fold several times.

2. Lay your picture on the folded cardboard. Mark the corners with a pencil.

3. Lay the picture on newspaper. Put glue on the back. Spread it from the middle to the edge.

4. Position the picture on the card, matching the pencil marks you made.

This small watercolor painting was mounted on colored paper before being glued on.

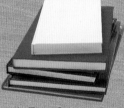

5. Place a clean sheet of paper over the picture and press it evenly all over.

6. Put the card under some books overnight. This ensures that the picture is flat.

The details on this card were added with a gold felt-tip pen.

This card was decorated with tissue paper shapes.

Frames

1. Cut a shape, bigger than your picture from thick cardboard.

2. Cut another piece of cardboard, the same size for a backing.

Press lightly.

3. Lay the picture on the first piece of cardboard. Use a pencil to draw around it.

Use a craft knife.

4. Draw lines ¼ in. inside the pencil line. Then, cut around the inside shape.

5. Tape the picture onto the frame. Glue the backing and press the frame onto it.

Decorate your frame before you tape the picture to it.

The frame above has little pieces of ripped tissue paper glued on it.

More ideas

On these pages and the next two pages, you will find lots more ideas which use techniques explained earlier in this part of the book.

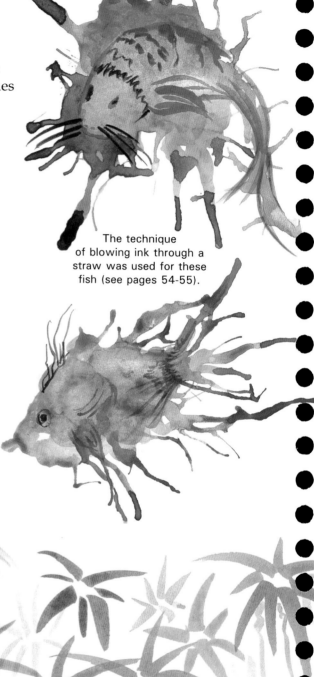

The technique of blowing ink through a straw was used for these fish (see pages 54-55).

The picture above has pieces of splattered paper glued together to make a collage (see pages 86-87).

The flowers and butterflies below, and hedgehog on page 93, have all been painted using different shades of ink (see page 42-43).

These dolphins were cut from tissue paper, then strips of tissue paper were glued on for waves (see pages 88-89).

The pictures above were done with tissue paper and acrylic paint (see pages 12-13).

The red and orange pattern on the right was painted with acrylic paints. The dots were added with a cotton swab (see pages 14-15).

This lion was done by blowing ink and then painting on top (see pages 54-55).

These flowers were masked out. Paint was sponged around the shapes instead of splattered (see pages 30-31).

These flowers and leaves are ripped from tissue paper, then glued onto paper (see pages 88-89).

To get a grainy effect like the one in the jungle scene and the two pictures below, sprinkle salt onto wet watercolor paint. (see pages 58-59).

This turtle is a collage of patterns scratched into thick acrylic paint (see pages 10-11).

This tree is a rubber band print (see pages 24-25).

This snail is another idea for using ripped tissue paper (see pages 88-89).

Shading ideas

This page shows you different ways of using lead pencils for filling in and shading your pictures.

Solid shading

The strength of your shading depends on the softness of the pencil you are using and how hard you press. The degree of softness is shown by an 'H' or 'B' number on the side of a pencil. H stands for hard, B stands for black.

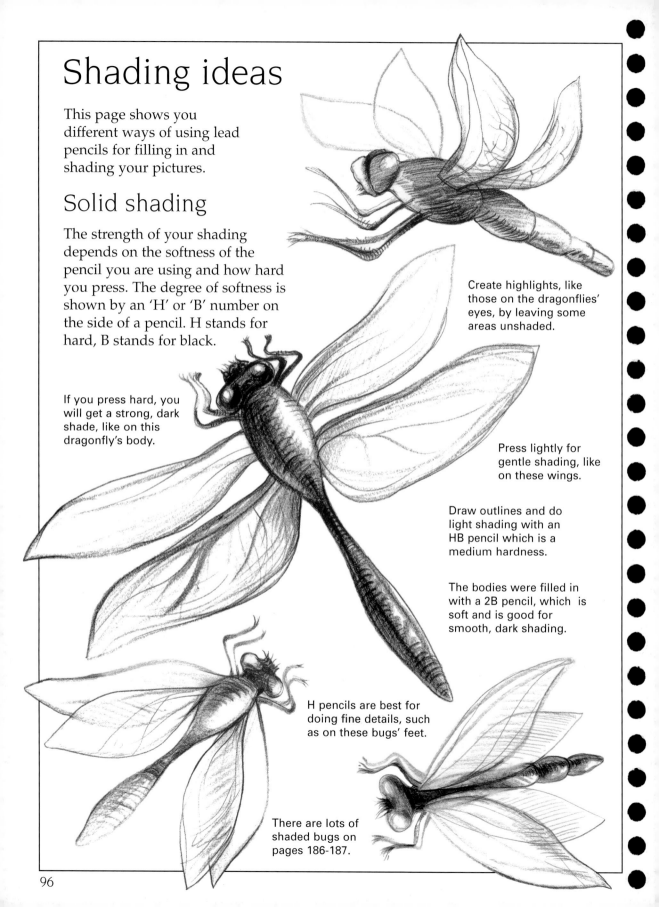

If you press hard, you will get a strong, dark shade, like on this dragonfly's body.

Create highlights, like those on the dragonflies' eyes, by leaving some areas unshaded.

Press lightly for gentle shading, like on these wings.

Draw outlines and do light shading with an HB pencil which is a medium hardness.

The bodies were filled in with a 2B pencil, which is soft and is good for smooth, dark shading.

H pencils are best for doing fine details, such as on these bugs' feet.

There are lots of shaded bugs on pages 186-187.

ART
skills

This picture is a
combination of several
ideas found in this book.

These trees were painted and
drawn using the techniques
on pages 116-119.

Find out on pages 112-113
how to print birds like the
little ones in the tree below.

These butterflies were drawn
with wax crayon, then filled
with paint (see pages 168-169).

Find out on pages
166-167 how to make
collage figures.

Materials

This double page gives you tips and reminders about how to use some of the art materials found in the projects which follow.

Paint

The types of paint used in the projects are watercolor paint, acrylic paint, poster paint and gouache.

Gouache and poster paints are quite thick and opaque. They can be used without mixing with water.

You'll find acrylic paint in tubes or bottles. Squeeze them onto an old plate or palette and add water to make them thinner and more transparent.

You can buy watercolor paints in tubes or in solid blocks called pans. Mix the paints with water before you use them.

This dog was painted with acrylic paint. See page 163 for this technique.

Pastels

There are several projects that use pastels, such as the resist technique on pages 104-105 and the landscape on pages 178-179.

Wax crayons can be substituted for oil pastels. They are good for rubbing and resist techniques.

Oil pastels

Oil pastels give a brighter effect than chalk pastels. Chalk pastels are good for techniques where colors are blended.

You'll find this scratched pastel technique on page 184.

Chalk pastels

Inks

Some of the ideas use colored inks, which come in bottles. You can also use the ink from a pen cartridge.

Pens

You'll also need a pen for some of the techniques. Felt-tip pens with permanent ink are ideal as they don't bleed, and they draw on top of most surfaces, including acrylic paint.

Permanent felt-tip pens are available in different colors and thickness.

Paper

Most of the examples in this section are shown at their real size, so this will give you an idea of the size of paper to use. It will tell you under the heading if you need a very large piece of paper

Thick watercolor paper that is 190gsm (90lb) or above won't wrinkle too much when you paint on it.

Hot-pressed watercolor paper has the smoothest surface. Rough watercolor paper has the most texture.

Bristol paper comes in pads or as individual sheets. It will wrinkle when you paint on it.

Different types of paper, such as colored writing paper, textured paper and old magazines are used for the techniques in this book.

Tissue paper flowers

BRISTOL PAPER OR THIN WHITE CARDBOARD

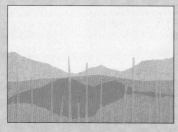

1. Rip some strips of blue tissue paper. Glue them across a piece of paper, making them overlap.

2. Cut some thin strips of green tissue paper for the stems and glue them at the bottom of the paper.

3. Cut out some red petals. Glue four petals around the top of some of the stems.

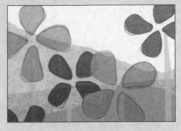

4. Cut out some orange petals. Glue them around other stems, overlapping some of the red petals.

5. Use a thin felt-tip pen to draw a line around each petal. It doesn't need to be too accurate.

6. Draw a small circle in the middle of each flower, then add two or three lines to each petal.

These flowers also have outlines drawn along their stems.

Reflections in water

GRAY OR ANOTHER PALE COLOR OF PAPER

1. Cut a large rectangle of gray paper, then fold it in half with its long sides together. Crease the fold then open the paper.

2. Use a white oil pastel to draw three thick lines above the fold. Draw lots of buildings, trees, street lights, a moon and stars.

3. Fold the paper again, then rub all over it with the back of a spoon. This transfers your drawing to the other half.

4. Open the paper. Paint the top half of the picture with dark blue ink or watercolor paint. The pastel will resist the paint.

5. Mix some water with the same color and paint it below the fold. Brush darker lines on top to make it look like water.

6. When it's dry, draw over the moon and lights with a yellow pastel. Fold the paper and rub over it to make yellow reflections.

Simple figures

THICK BRIGHT PAPER OR CARDBOARD

1. Cut a piece of thick paper or cardboard. Rip a rectangle from some brown butcher paper and glue it in the middle.

2. Rip a slightly wider rectangle from a bright piece of tissue paper and glue it over the brown butcher paper.

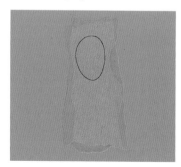

3. When the glue has dried, use a water-based felt-tip pen or a fountain pen to draw an oval for the face.

4. Draw two lines for the neck and a round-necked T-shirt. Add lines for the arms, but don't worry about drawing hands.

5. Draw a curved line for the eyebrow and nose, then add the other eyebrow and eyes. Draw the ears, hair and lips.

6. Then, dip a paintbrush into some clean water. Paint the water along some of the lines to make the ink run a little.

7. Rip a rough T-shirt shape from tissue paper and glue it over your drawing. Add a torn paper stripe, too.

8. Finally, when the glue has dried, paint thin stripes across the T-shirt using a bright color of watercolor paint.

Fantasy castle

BRISTOL PAPER OR THIN CARDBOARD

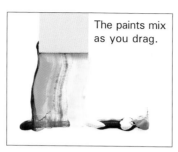

The paints mix as you drag.

1. Squeeze a line of acrylic paint along the bottom of the paper, straight from the tube. Use blue, turquoise and white.

2. Cut pieces of thick cardboard, making them different widths. Place a piece below the paint, then drag it upward.

3. Then, use the other pieces of cardboard to drag more towers, making them different heights. Leave it to dry.

4. Put some black paint onto a plate and dip the edge of another piece of cardboard into it. Drag it over the dried paint.

5. Dip the edge of the cardboard into the black paint again and use it to print lines for bridges between the towers.

6. Dip a narrow piece of cardboard into the paint. Drag small rectangles under the towers, to give them shadows.

7. When the paint has dried, use a black felt-tip pen to draw bridges, trees, turrets, windows and weather vanes.

This sunset scene was created using the same technique.

Small birds were drawn
around these towers to
give the towers a
sense of scale.

Tissue paper fruit

TISSUE PAPER

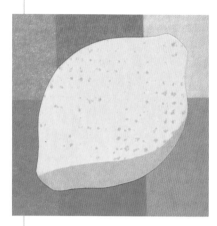

Try using different sides of the grater to get different textures.

Orange

1. Cut a circle from orange tissue paper. Then, cut a curved strip of tissue paper and glue it along one side.

2. Lay the tissue paper orange on a grater. Then, rub the side of an orange oil pastel or wax crayon gently over the paper.

3. Continue rubbing until the orange is covered with texture. Then, use a fine black felt-tip pen to add a stalk to the top.

Apple

Cut an apple shape from green tissue paper. Rub it with a green pastel around one side and at the top. Glue on a stalk.

Lemon

Cut a lemon from yellow tissue paper. Glue a green strip along one edge. Rub it with a yellow oil pastel, then a light green one.

Lime

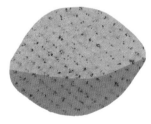

Cut the shape of a lime from green tissue paper. Add a green strip along one edge, then rub it all over with a green pastel.

This background was made by overlapping rectangles of tissue paper.

Strawberry

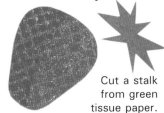

Cut a stalk from green tissue paper.

Cut a strawberry from red tissue paper. Add a red strip covering about half of the shape. Rub it with a yellow oil pastel.

Grapefruit

Cut a circle from yellow tissue paper and add a pale green strip. Rub it with a yellow, then a light green pastel. Add a stalk.

Pear

Add a stalk.

Cut a pear shape from green tissue paper. Rub down one side with a green pastel. Then, glue on a stalk.

Printed birds in a tree

ANY TYPE OF THICK PAPER

1. For the branches, pour some brown poster paint onto an old plate, then dip the edge of a strip of thick cardboard into it.

2. Press the painted edge onto your paper. Dip the cardboard into the paint, then print another branch, joining the first one.

The bodies and heads of these birds were printed at different angles to make them look animated.

You don't need this half.

3. Dip different widths of cardboard into the paint and print more branches. Leave spaces between them for the birds.

4. While the branches are drying, cut a small potato in half, lengthways. Then, cut one piece in half again.

5. For the birds' bodies, spread red paint on some paper towels. Press the cut side of one of the pieces of potato onto it.

6. Print a body onto the paper, with the straight edge at the top. Print more bodies in the spaces between the branches.

7. For the tails, dip the edge of some cardboard into the paint. Put it at the end of the body and twist it. Fingerprint the heads.

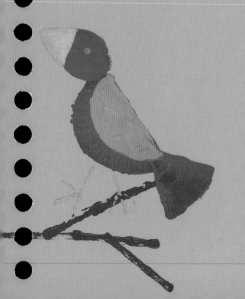

8. For the wings, cut a slice off the other small piece of potato. Press it in orange paint and print it on the body.

9. Paint a yellow beak and a blue eye on each bird. Then, paint short yellow lines for the legs, using a thin brush.

113

Paper shapes

ANY KIND OF COLORED PAPER

Spiral

1. Cut a circle from colored paper, then draw a spiral from the edge of the circle to the middle of it.

2. At the middle of the circle, curve the line around a little, then draw another line out to the edge of the circle.

3. Cut along one of the lines of the spiral, turning the paper as you cut. Continue cutting until you reach the edge again.

4. Cut the pointed end off the spiral and trim any wobbly bits from around the edges. Glue it onto another color of paper.

Build up layers of different shapes on top of each other.

For a sun, cut a circle, then cut small triangles out of its edge. Glue another circle on top.

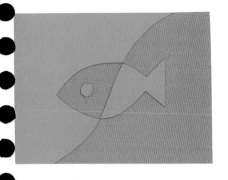

The shapes below
could be used on a
Valentine's card.

Try combining
rounded
shapes with
squares and
rectangles.

Fish

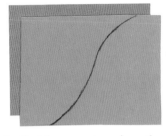

1. Cut two rectangles, the
same size, from blue and
orange paper. Then, draw
a wavy line across the
blue one.

2. Draw a simple outline
of a fish across the line.
Cut along the line, then
cut out the front part of
the fish, like this.

3. Glue the front part
onto the orange rectangle.
Then, cut out the back of
the blue fish and glue it
on. Glue on a blue eye.

Techniques for trees

The next four pages show you lots of different ways of drawing, painting and printing trees. When you try any of these techniques, you will get a better result if you make your tree bigger than the ones shown.

This oil painting of olive trees, by Vincent van Gogh, was painted in 1889. Van Gogh used lots of short lines to build up the shape and color of the trees and the sky.

Oil pastel trees

1. Draw a twisted tree trunk using dark brown oil pastels. Add several short branches.

This tree was filled in with dots, instead of short lines.

2. Draw lots of short diagonal lines with a green oil pastel, overlapping the branches.

3. Add more diagonal lines for the leaves, using a lighter green and a lime green pastel.

Use orange, brown and rusty pastels for fall leaves on a tree.

Pen and ink

1. Use brown ink to paint a very simple trunk with three thick branches coming from it.

2. Use green ink to paint a wavy line for the top of the tree. Then fill it in, leaving some small gaps.

3. Use a felt-tip or an ink pen to draw loopy lines around the edge of the tree and around the gaps.

Brushed branches

1. Paint a patch of green and brown watercolor paint. Splatter it by flicking the bristles of your brush.

2. Leave it to dry, then use different shades of brown watercolor paint to paint the trunk.

3. While the trunk is still wet, paint the branches by brushing the paint up onto the leaves.

Chalk pastel leaves

1. Paint a trunk with yellowy-brown watercolor paint. Add some branches, too.

2. Draw lines using a light green chalk pastel. Add some darker green lines on top.

3. Gently rub the tip of your little finger down the lines to smudge the chalks together.

More techniques for trees

Sponged leaves

Use a natural sponge if you have one.

1. Use the tip of a brush to paint the trunk and twisted branches of a tree, using watercolor paint or ink.

2. Dampen a piece of sponge, then dip it into some red paint. Dab it gently around the tops of the branches.

3. Wash the sponge, then squeeze as much water out as you can. Dip it into purple paint, then dab it around the branches.

This tree was blow-painted through a straw (see pages 152-153). Use this technique for a tree in winter.

Dip the hard end of a paintbrush in paint, then drag it across a patch of wet watercolor paint to make branches.

The leaves on this tree were printed with an eraser which had been cut into leaf shapes (see page 144 for this technique).

Zigzag trees

Use the tip of the brush.

1. Paint three tree trunks using green watercolor paint. Make them get thinner toward the top. Add some ground.

2. Put the tip of your brush at the top of a tree and paint a zigzag down the trunk. Make it get wider as you paint.

3. Continue painting, but leave part of the trunk showing at the bottom. Then, zigzag some clean water over the top.

Draw a trunk with brown chalk pastels. Scribble pastels for the leaves. Smudge them in a few places.

This stylized tree was drawn with chalk pastels. The leaves were drawn first then the trunk was added.

These leaves were painted first in dark green acrylic, then lighter green was added on top.

119

Sponge-printed snails

ANY TYPE OF PAPER

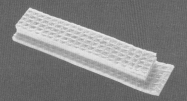

This is the end you print with.

1. Cut a piece of kitchen sponge 6½ x 1½ in. and two pieces 6 x 1in. Lay them together, matching the top edges, like this.

2. Cut a long piece of tape, so that it is ready to use. Fold the end of the long piece of sponge over the end of the shorter pieces.

3. Roll up the pieces of sponge carefully but not too tightly, keeping the edges even. Secure the sponge with the tape.

4. Pour blue acrylic paint onto an old plate and spread it a little. Then, dip the end of the sponge into the paint.

5. Print spirals all over a piece of paper. Press the sponge into the paint again each time you print a spiral.

6. When the paint is dry, paint a snail's body below each spiral. Then, use a thin paintbrush to paint the antennae.

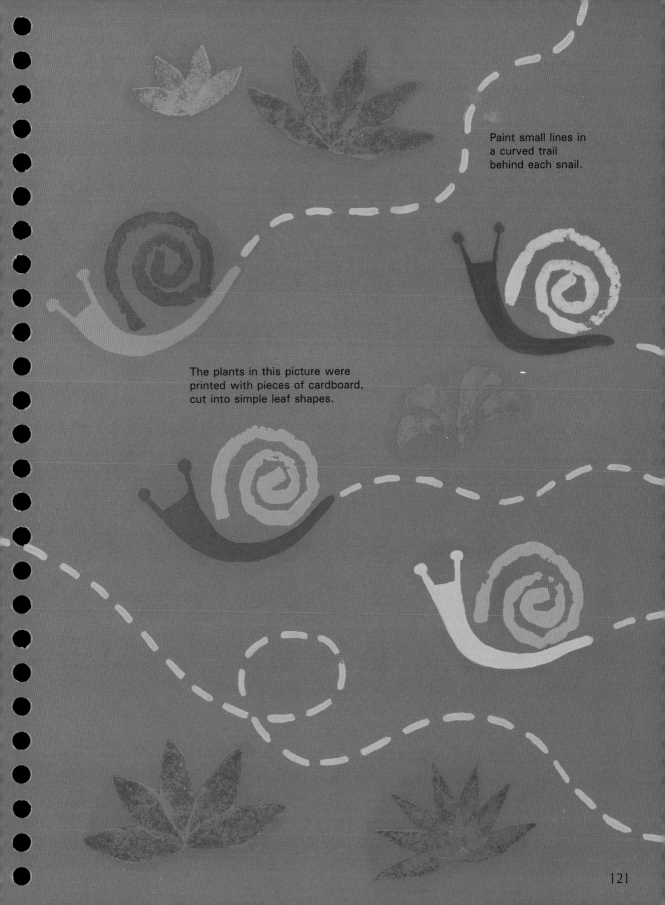

Paint small lines in
a curved trail
behind each snail.

The plants in this picture were
printed with pieces of cardboard,
cut into simple leaf shapes.

Fingerpainted flowers

BRISTOL PAPER OR THIN CARDBOARD

Drag your finger toward
the middle each time.

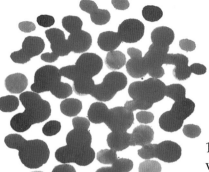

The stem, leaves and
pot of this flower
were painted with a
brush, then the
flower head was
fingerpainted on top.

1. Use a brush to paint a
vase using poster paint or
acrylic paint. When the
paint is dry, fingerpaint
some dots on the vase.

2. For a daffodil, dip a
fingertip in yellow paint.
Then, drag six lines for
the petals, making them
join in the middle.

3. Do several more
daffodils above the vase.
When the paint is dry,
fingerpaint a star shape in
the middle of the petals.

4. For a tulip, fingerpaint
a curved line with bright
red paint. Do another line
that meets the first one at
the bottom.

5. For the blue flowers,
dip a fingertip in paint
and print a small dot.
Add lots more dots in a
rough triangular shape.

6. To complete the flower
arrangement, use a
paintbrush to paint green
leaves in the spaces
between the flowers.

The yellow background in this picture was painted first, with a gap left for the vase. The vase was painted overlapping the yellow slightly.

Oil pastel lizards

ANY THICK WHITE PAPER

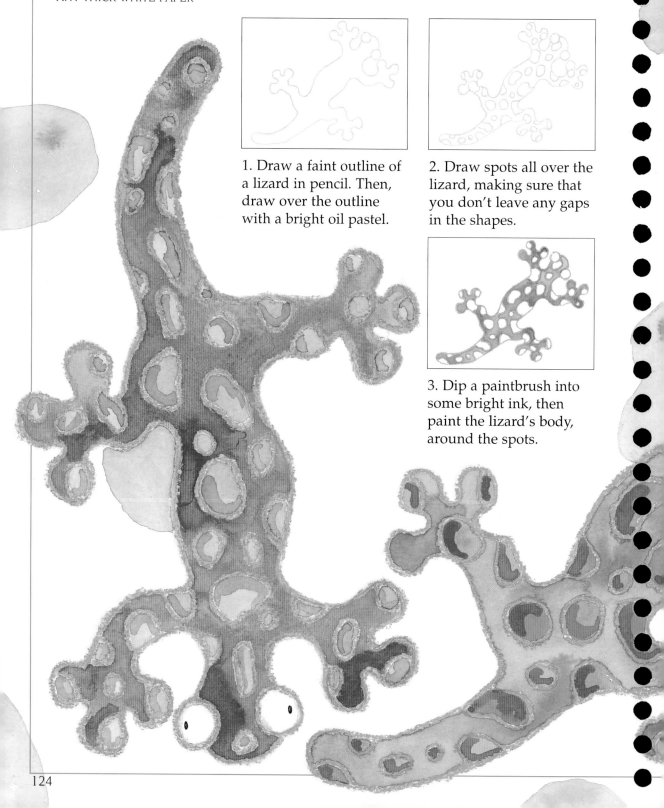

1. Draw a faint outline of a lizard in pencil. Then, draw over the outline with a bright oil pastel.

2. Draw spots all over the lizard, making sure that you don't leave any gaps in the shapes.

3. Dip a paintbrush into some bright ink, then paint the lizard's body, around the spots.

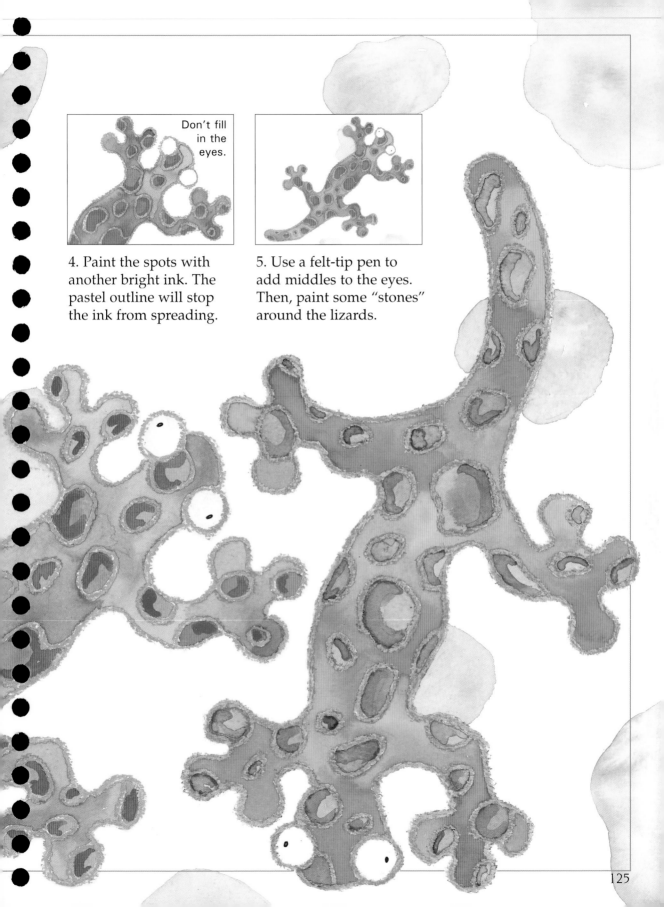

Don't fill in the eyes.

4. Paint the spots with another bright ink. The pastel outline will stop the ink from spreading.

5. Use a felt-tip pen to add middles to the eyes. Then, paint some "stones" around the lizards.

Textured houses

THICK WHITE CARDBOARD

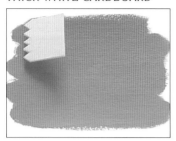

1. Cut a zigzag at one end of a strip of cardboard. Then, paint a rectangle of acrylic paint on another piece of cardboard.

2. Drag the zigzag end of the cardboard across the paint again and again to make textured lines. Leave the paint to dry.

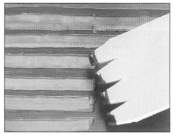

3. Cut several small triangles into the end of another cardboard strip. Drag it across another rectangle of paint.

4. For a very fine texture, drag the end of an old toothbrush across a rectangle of paint, again and again.

5. Do some more textured patches of paint by experimenting with different shapes cut into strips of cardboard.

6. Cut rectangles from the textures for the buildings, windows, doors and roofs. Glue them on another piece of cardboard.

Patterned reptiles

BRISTOL PAPER OR WATERCOLOR PAPER

Instead of painting patterns, you could paint tiny triangles along the back and tail of the reptile.

1. Use ink to paint a body. Then, without lifting the brush, use less and less pressure, to paint a curling tail.

Paint a blue dot in the eye.

2. Dip the brush in the ink again and paint a head and a front and back leg. Add three "fingers" to each leg.

3. When the ink is dry, add green poster paint dots to the body and let them dry. Then, add little yellow dots on top.

4. For the crocodile, use ink to paint a long wavy line. Paint over one side of it again with the same color, to make a shadow.

5. Paint shapes for the head and legs. When the ink has dried, add two eyes with white poster paint.

Add middles to the eyes with blue paint.

6. Paint yellow triangles on the body and outline the eyes. Then, when the paint has dried, fill them in with pale blue paint.

These snakes were painted using one long brushstroke for the bodies.

Don't worry if the patterns overlap the edges of your creatures.

Techniques for skies

On the next four pages you will find different techniques and tips for drawing and painting skies and clouds. Watercolor paints are very good for creating atmospheric skies.

This picture, called *Rain, Steam and Speed*, was painted in oil paints by J.M.W. Turner in 1844. The sky is stormy, but Turner painted bright areas on some of the clouds, which makes it look as if the sun is about to break through.

Watery clouds

1. Brush clean water onto a piece of watercolor paper. Then, use the tip of a brush to blob on patches of blue watercolor paint.

2. The paint will run. Then, press the brush a little bit more firmly in some places to make darker patches of sky.

Summer sky

1. Mix enough cobalt blue watercolor paint to cover a piece of watercolor paper. Paint a stripe across the top.

2. Paint another stripe below the first one before it has had a chance to dry. Paint quickly and make the stripes overlap.

3. Continue painting overlapping stripes all the way down the paper. This technique is known as 'painting a wash'.

4. Before the paint has dried, scrunch up a paper towel and dab it in several areas on the paper to lift some paint off.

5. When the paint has dried, mix some darker blue. Paint it along the bottom of each cloud to make shadows.

More techniques for skies

Rainy sky

1. Wet some watercolor paper with clean water. Then, mix Prussian blue watercolor paint with brown to make dark gray.

2. Paint overlapping stripes across the top of the paper. They don't need to be even or to start in the same place.

3. While the paint is still quite wet, add blue stripes across the middle, then gray ones at the bottom of the paper.

4. Before the paint has dried, swipe a cotton swab across the paint so that the bottom is almost white. Leave it to dry.

5. While it is drying, practice painting some fine lines for the rain, using gray paint on a piece of scrap paper.

6. When your painting is completely dry, paint fine lines for the rain, coming from the gray area near the top of the paper.

Starry night

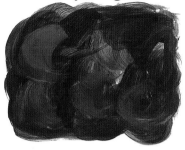

1. Paint a piece of cardboard with dark blue acrylic paint. Move the brush around in a circle to get an uneven finish.

2. When the paint is dry, paint some planets with pale yellow acrylic paint. Then, add several stars around them.

3. For the tiny stars, dip a paintbrush into the yellow paint, then splatter it all over, following the steps on page 169.

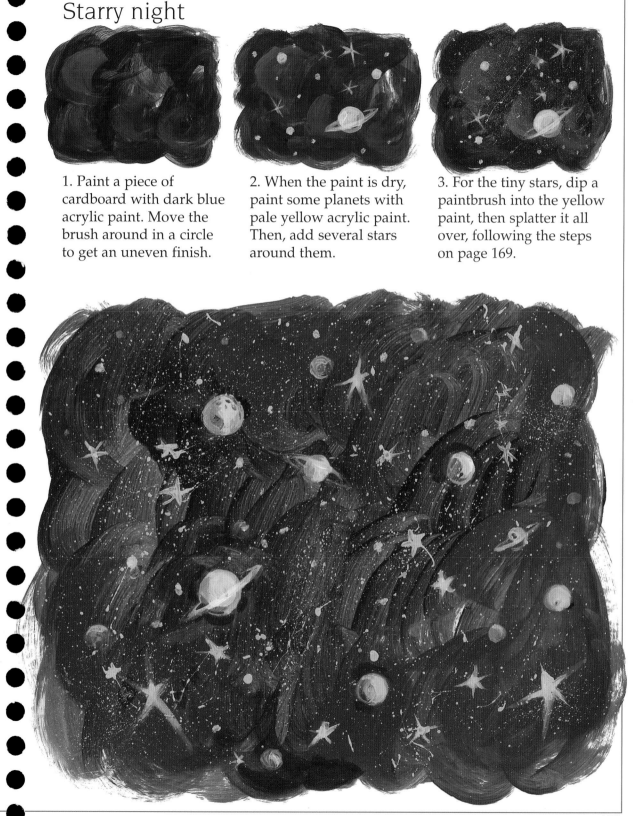

Leaf collage
THICK PAPER OR CARDBOARD

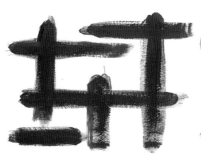

1. Use dark paint and a thick paintbrush to paint vertical and horizontal lines on your paper.

2. When the paint has dried, cut a piece of tissue paper to cover the lines, and glue it on.

3. Rip some squares and rectangles from different colors of tissue paper and glue them on.

4. Cut a square of corrugated cardboard. Press it into some paint and print it several times.

5. Either cut out leaves from a picture in a magazine, or cut some leaf shapes from paper.

6. Cut small rectangles from a magazine picture of leaves or grass. Glue them on.

7. Add some horizontal and vertical lines with a felt-tip pen. Then, outline the leaves, loosely.

Doodle painting
BROWN BUTCHER PAPER

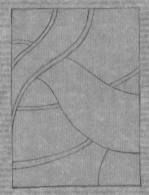

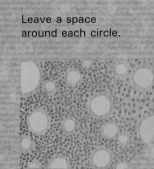

Leave a space
around each circle.

1. Use a pencil to draw a rectangle on some brown butcher paper. Draw curving lines to separate the rectangle into sections.

2. In one section, paint pale blue spots a little way apart. Fill in the spaces around them with lots of darker blue dots.

3. Paint white circles, one inside another. Add purple, blue and yellow inside them. Fill around the circles in light blue.

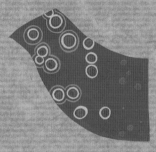

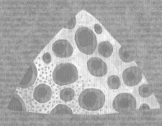

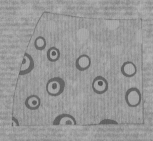

4. Fill one section with blue. When it's dry, add purple spots, then paint yellow and light blue circles around them.

5. In another section, paint blue spots. Fill in around them with white paint, leaving a space. Add tiny blue dots.

6. Paint light blue spots. Outline them in darker blue, then add a purple dot. Add a circle of pale blue dots around each one.

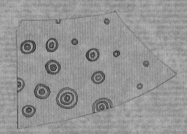

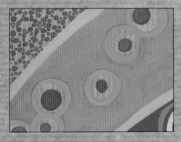

7. Use the tip of a thin brush to paint small purple circles. Paint more circles around them, leaving gaps in between.

8. Then, fill in the spaces between the circles with curved lines, following the shapes of the circles, like this.

9. Fill in the rest of the sections with different patterns of circles, spots and dots. Fill in thick lines between some sections.

Random patterns

THICK BRISTOL OR WATERCOLOR PAPER

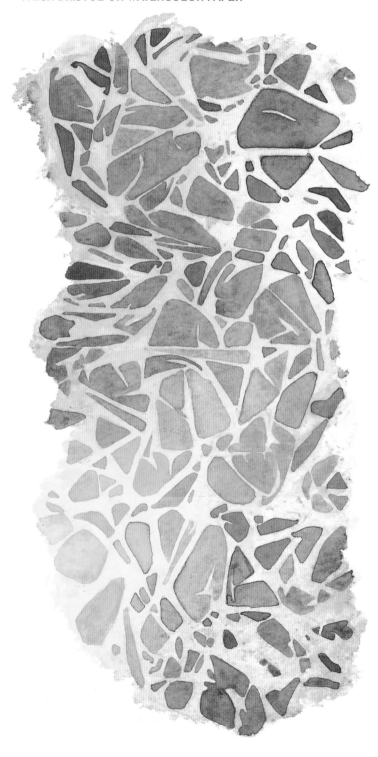

1. Mix different colors of watercolor paint. Make them quite watery. Paint them in patches close to each other.

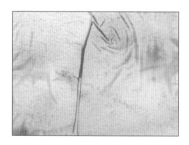

2. Before the paint has dried, cut a piece of plastic foodwrap larger than your painting. Then, lay it over the paint.

3. Use your fingers to move the paint under the foodwrap, to make patterns and blend the colors together.

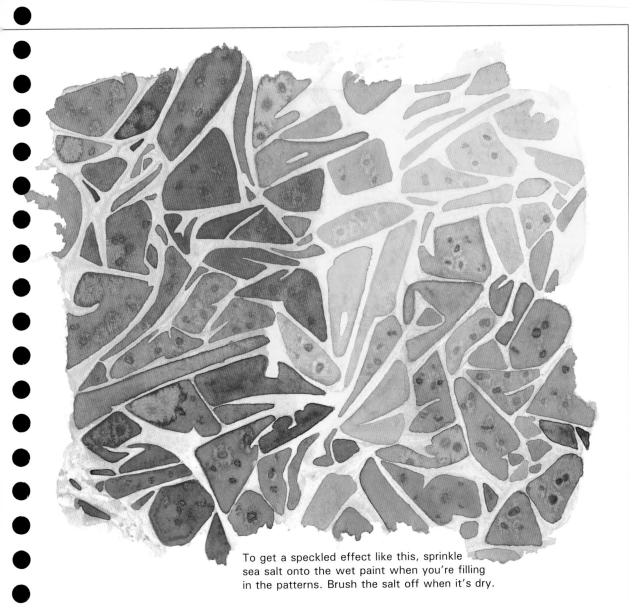

To get a speckled effect like this, sprinkle sea salt onto the wet paint when you're filling in the patterns. Brush the salt off when it's dry.

4. Leave the foodwrap on top of the paint and let the paint dry completely. Then, carefully peel off the foodwrap.

5. Use watercolor paints to fill in lots of the patterns left by the foodwrap. Leave a space around each shape.

6. Continue filling in the patterns using some strong colors and some paler ones. Leave some of the patterns unfilled.

Fall leaves

WATERCOLOR PAPER

1. Mix a little red and yellow watercolor paint to make orange. Paint it evenly across the bottom of the paper, like this.

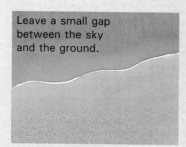

Leave a small gap between the sky and the ground.

2. Mix lots of Prussian blue watercolor paint with water. Paint across the top of the paper for the sky.

3. Before the sky has dried, dip a paintbrush into water, then let it drip onto the sky. The paint will spread a little.

4. Mix red and green acrylic paint to make brown. Drag your brush down several times to paint the tree trunk.

5. Add some branches in the same way, then use a thinner paintbrush to paint finer twigs at the ends of the branches.

6. When the paint is dry, use a brown oil pastel or wax crayon to draw wavy lines for the middle veins of the leaves.

7. Mix red and yellow watercolor paint to make shades of orange. Paint a leaf shape around each line.

8. Paint a few little leaves on the tree and some in the sky. This will make it look as if the leaves are blowing in the wind.

9. When all the leaves are dry, use a fine brush to paint lots of thin, dark brown lines on each of the large leaves.

This picture was painted on
rough watercolor paper
which gives the background
a grainy texture.

141

Tissue paper pond

TISSUE PAPER

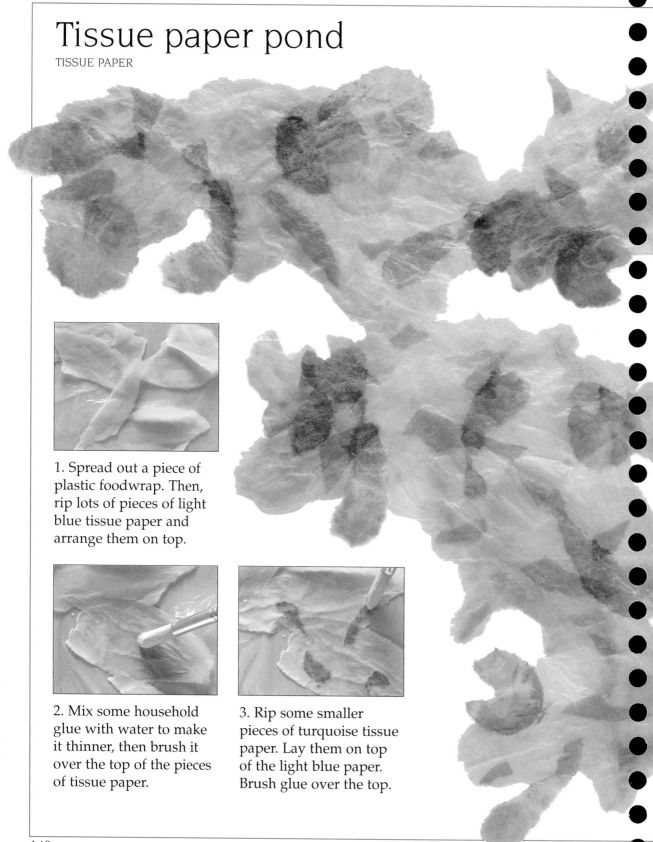

1. Spread out a piece of plastic foodwrap. Then, rip lots of pieces of light blue tissue paper and arrange them on top.

2. Mix some household glue with water to make it thinner, then brush it over the top of the pieces of tissue paper.

3. Rip some smaller pieces of turquoise tissue paper. Lay them on top of the light blue paper. Brush glue over the top.

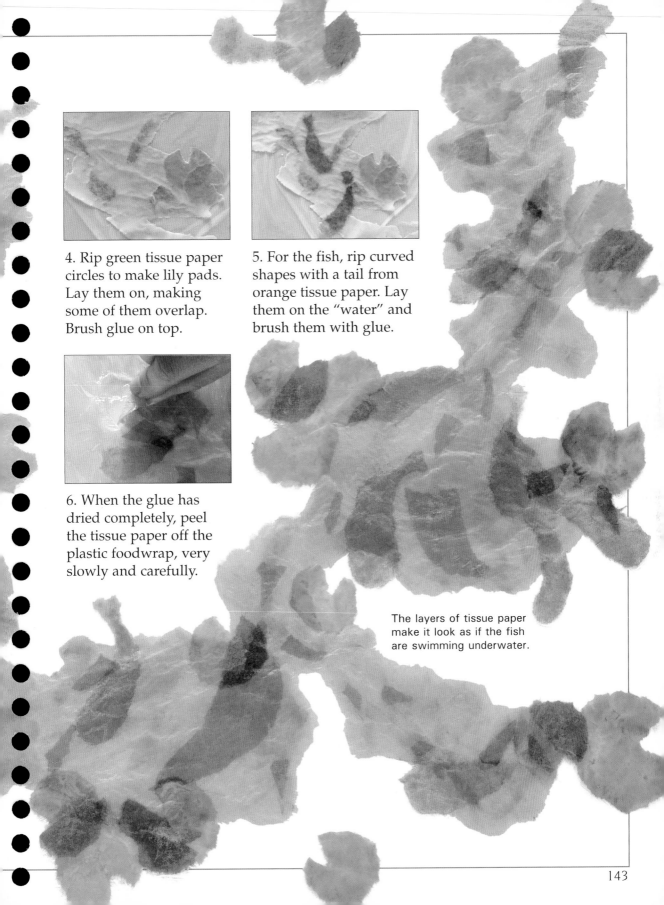

4. Rip green tissue paper circles to make lily pads. Lay them on, making some of them overlap. Brush glue on top.

5. For the fish, rip curved shapes with a tail from orange tissue paper. Lay them on the "water" and brush them with glue.

6. When the glue has dried completely, peel the tissue paper off the plastic foodwrap, very slowly and carefully.

The layers of tissue paper make it look as if the fish are swimming underwater.

Geometric prints

ANY PAPER

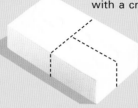

Be very careful when cutting with a craft knife.

1. Use a craft knife to cut a long eraser in half. Then, cut one of the pieces of eraser in half lengthways.

2. Draw sets of parallel lines along the eraser. Then, holding the knife at an angle, make a clean cut along one line.

3. Turn the eraser around and cut along the other side of the line to make a groove. Cut the other line in the same way.

4. Cut the corners off the other half of the eraser to make a triangle. Draw four lines on it, then cut along them as before.

5. Push a map pin or an ordinary pin into the back of both pieces of eraser. This makes them easier to hold when you print.

6. Wet a piece of sponge cloth, then squeeze out as much water as you can. Spread acrylic paint on it with the back of a spoon.

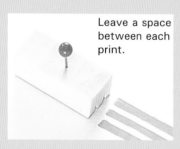

Leave a space between each print.

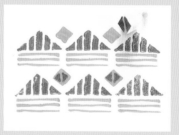

7. Press the first eraser into the paint, then onto some paper. Press it in the paint again before you do another print.

8. Then, do a triangle print above each set of line prints. Repeat these rows of prints several times on your paper.

9. Cut a small square of eraser and print it between each triangle. Then, cut a line across another square of eraser and print it on top.

These geometric patterns were built up using erasers cut into different shapes.

Techniques for water

On the next four pages you will find different techniques for drawing and painting water. There are ideas for waves, rippling water and reflections of moonlight on water.

This photograph of a crashing wave shows different shapes, patterns and colors which can be found in water.

Soapy painting

Use a brush with stiff bristles.

1. Dip a brush into some blue watercolor paint. Then, move the bristles around on an old bar of soap.

2. Paint the soapy paint straight onto a piece of watercolor paper, moving the brush in a wavy pattern.

3. Dip the brush into a different shade of blue paint and then on the soap again. Paint more waves, overlapping them.

The soap helps to show the marks made by the paintbrush.

4. Paint a boat with thick red and blue watercolor paint. Add an outline with a fine felt-tip pen.

Oil pastel squiggles

1. Use a brown oil pastel to draw some rounded rocks on a piece of Bristol paper. Shade them in, like this.

2. Then, draw squiggles around the rocks with a turquoise oil pastel. Leave some spaces between them.

3. Add a dark blue pastel shadow beneath each rock and add more squiggles. Draw a turquoise reflection on each rock.

Painted ripples

1. Dampen a piece of watercolor paper with clean water. Then, paint it with blue watercolor paint, leaving some gaps.

2. When the paint is dry, paint wavy lines with a darker blue paint. Add some even darker ones with the tip of a brush.

More techniques for water
Sea collage

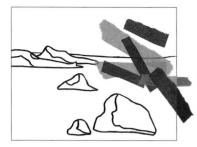

1. Draw some rocks on some thick cardboard and add a line for the horizon. Then, rip strips of blue tissue paper.

2. Paint the sky with blue acrylic paint. When the sky is dry, glue pieces of pale blue paper around the rocks for the sea.

3. Glue on some darker shades of blue paper. Rip paper shapes for rocks and glue them on. Add tissue paper shadows.

4. For the waves, glue on pieces of white tissue paper. Dab white acrylic or poster paint along the top of each wave.

5. Dip your brush in the paint again, then splatter it over the top of a wave by following steps 5 and 6 on page 169.

Wax resist reflections

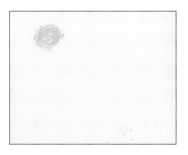

1. Draw a moon with a white oil pastel on watercolor paper. It's shown here in yellow so that you can see it.

2. Add lots of short lines, starting about a third of the way down the paper. Make each line a little longer than the one before.

3. Use darkish blue watercolor paint to paint a line of distant hills between the moon and the lines on the water.

4. Then paint the sky and the water with yellow watercolor. Use a tissue to lift patches of paint off the sky, for clouds.

5. When the paint is dry, paint a strip of land. Paint a tree trunk, then dab on leaves with the tip of a brush and a sponge.

Ink and pastel pets

WATERCOLOR PAPER

The ink will run on the paper.

1. Use a clean sponge or a wide paintbrush to wet a piece of watercolor paper.

2. Dip a thick paintbrush into some bright ink and paint lines for the head, ear, body, legs and tail.

3. While the ink is still wet, use the tip of a brush to add spots. Do one on the head for the eye.

Fill in around the dog with another color of ink.

4. When it's dry, outline the body with a black felt-tip pen. Add a nose, eyes and lines on the paws.

5. Draw on a few dots and hairs, too. Fill in the nose and draw a collar with chalk pastels.

In this picture, the roof was drawn after the cat.

Cat

1. Paint a curve for a cat's back on wet watercolor paper. Add a head, legs and a line for a tail.

2. When the ink is dry, draw stripes on the body, legs and tail with a chalk pastel.

Fill in the ears and nose, too.

3. Use a felt-tip pen to draw an outline. Add claws and whiskers too. Add eyes with a pastel.

Blow-painted trees

THICK BRISTOL PAPER OR WATERCOLOR PAPER

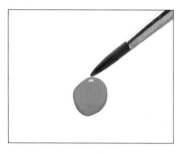

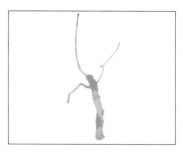

1. Dip a paintbrush into some bright ink and paint a thick blob for the tree trunk.

2. Blow through a drinking straw so that you extend the ink up the paper for the trunk.

3. Then, use the end of the straw to pull little lines of ink away from the trunk.

Drag little wisps of grass with the tip of a paintbrush.

You may
need to add
more ink.

4. Blow the lines of ink to make the branches. Then, paint and blow more trees in the same way.

5. For the leaves, mix orange ink with water. Dab it over the branches again and again.

6. For the ground, mix more watery ink and paint it around the bottom of the trees.

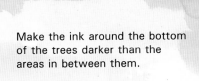

Make the ink around the bottom of the trees darker than the areas in between them.

Domed buildings

THICK BRISTOL PAPER OR WATERCOLOR PAPER

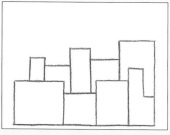

1. Use a pencil to draw several large rectangles on your paper. Make them different sizes.

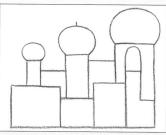

2. Add some domes and turrets. Make them different sizes and shapes, too.

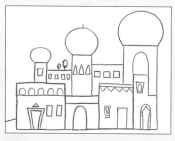

3. Add lots of different shapes of windows, doorways, columns and arches to the buildings.

4. Use watercolor paints or inks to fill in the buildings. Leave a small gap between each part.

5. When the paint or ink is dry, fill in the domes with a gold felt-tip pen or gold paint.

6. Draw around some of the windows and add patterns to the buildings, with a gold pen.

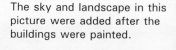

The sky and landscape in this picture were added after the buildings were painted.

155

Animal shapes

THIN CARDBOARD

Tessellating bird

1. Cut a corner off a square of thin cardboard then, tape the triangle along the top edge of the square, like this.

2. Cut the other bottom corner off the square and tape it along the top, so that the two triangles meet in the middle.

3. To make the beak, cut a long v-shape into the left-hand side. Tape the shape onto the triangle at the top.

Shapes like these, which fit together exactly to form repeating patterns, are called tessellations.

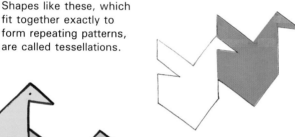 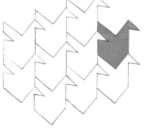

4. Draw around the bird shape. Then, move the shape so that the beak fits under the wing. Draw around it again.

5. Continue drawing around the shape so that you build up a pattern of birds which fit into each other on all sides.

These birds were painted with gouache, then outlined with a black felt-tip pen.

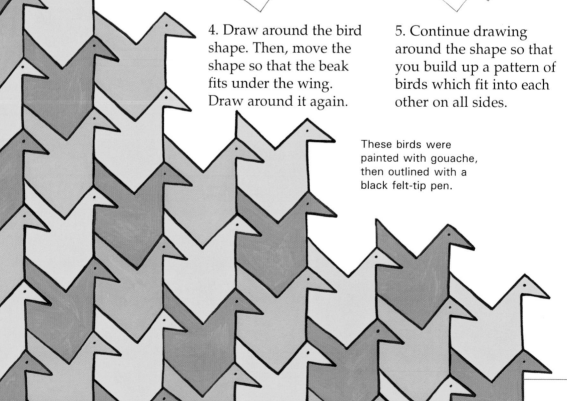

Transformations

1. Draw a row of five tall triangles and fill them in. Add four triangles above them, making their sides curve slightly.

2. Draw three white curvy triangles in the spaces. Add more blue ones and white ones on top. Make the shapes curve, like this.

3. Draw two blue shapes which look like sitting seals. Then, draw several swimming seals. Add flippers and eyes.

The shapes gradually transform, or change, from one thing into another.

Street scene

A PIECE OF THIN CARDBOARD

1. Make a pale apricot color by mixing white and orange acrylic paint. Brush it all over a large piece of cardboard.

2. When the paint has dried, paint a blue shape for the cab of a truck. Paint a brown tank and add green wheels.

3. Use the apricot paint to add windows and headlights. Paint a curve on the tank, and two small tanks below. Let it dry.

To do a street scene like this, paint rough shapes for the signs, dog, and so on, before you do the outlines. Then draw some people.

 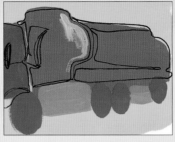 

4. Without lifting your pen, outline the whole cab with a black felt-tip pen. You may need to go over some lines twice.

5. Continue the line onto the brown tank. Draw a shape for the flat part at the front of the tank, then outline the back part.

6. Continue the line around and around for the wheels and along the two small tanks under the truck, too.

Techniques for fur

Some animals have long hairy fur, curly fur, or smooth skin. They can also be one color or have amazing patterned fur. Here are a few suggestions of different ways to draw animal fur:

The long fur on these animals called guanacos was painted with lots of thin wavy lines. Shorter, straighter lines have been used on the smooth fur.

Use a soft 4B or 6B pencil to draw an animal with skin rather than fur, like this elephant.

Use the tip of a brush to soften patterns on fur.

For hairy fur, add fine wavy hairs with chalk pastels.

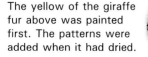

Press harder and harder with a pencil for fur like this.

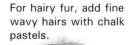

The yellow of the giraffe fur above was painted first. The patterns were added when it had dried.

The spots and hair of this spotted fur were drawn on a patch of orange chalk pastel.

Pencil and paint

1. Use a soft 6B pencil to draw a lion's eyes, ears and nose. Add some curved lines for the mane.

2. Paint lines in shades of orange between the pencil lines, but don't put too much paint on your brush.

Add some shading down the side of the face and over the eyes when the paint is dry.

Chalk pastel leopard

1. Use a pencil to draw a faint outline of a leopard on colored paper. Fill in its nose and eyes and add some long whiskers.

2. Using a chalk pastel, fill in areas on the leopard's head, along the neck and back, and down the legs and tail.

3. Use a darker pastel to fill in shadows under the chin and on the tail, legs and tummy. Smudge the pastel with a finger.

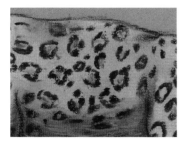

4. Add spots on the head, back, tail and legs. Then, outline the leopard and its eyes and nose with a black pastel.

More techniques for fur

Watercolor seal

1. Draw the outline of a seal's body with a pencil on watercolor paper. Add the flippers.

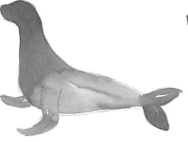

2. Fill in your outline with blue watercolor paint. Use Prussian blue if you have it.

3. Before the paint has dried, lift off a line of paint along the body with a tissue or a dry brush.

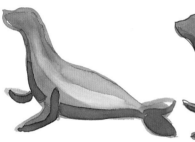

4. Paint darker blue lines for shadows along the neck, flippers, tummy, and on the tail.

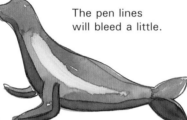

The pen lines will bleed a little.

5. Before the lines have dried, outline the seal with a water-based felt-tip pen.

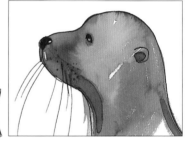

6. Use the pen to add an eye, ear and nose. Draw some dots on the chin and add long whiskers.

The different shades of blue help to make the seals' fur look sleek and smooth.

This dog's tail has been printed more than once. It makes it look as if it's wagging.

Dragged paint dogs

Make sure you have lots of paint on your brush.

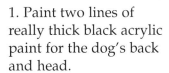

1. Paint two lines of really thick black acrylic paint for the dog's back and head.

2. Use the edge of a piece of cardboard to drag the paint downward to make the head and body.

3. Use the corner of the cardboard to drag the paint to make the ears, legs and tail.

Use a ballpoint or felt-tip pen.

4. When the paint is dry, draw wavy lines under the head and body. Add lines to the ears and feet.

5. Draw a curved line for a collar around the dog's neck with a bright chalk pastel or oil pastel.

6. Then, use a craft knife to scratch vertical lines into the paint on the dog's head and body.

Wet paper watercolor

WATERCOLOR PAPER

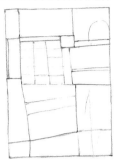

1. Do a plan on some scrap paper before you start. Draw a rectangle and fill it with shapes, like this.

2. Paint a rectangle of watercolor paper with clean water. Following your plan, fill in the main shapes with pale colors.

3. When the paint has dried, fill some of the shapes with a stronger color. Paint patterns in some of the shapes.

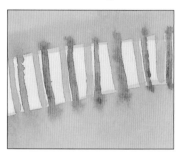

4. While the paint is still wet, add small lines in different colors, letting the paints bleed into each other.

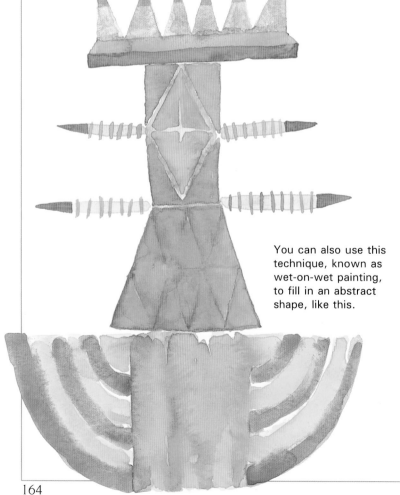

You can also use this technique, known as wet-on-wet painting, to fill in an abstract shape, like this.

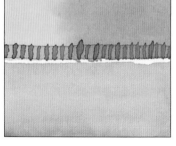

5. When the paint has dried, paint some more little lines. The colors won't bleed as they did when the paint was wet.

Town collage

BRISTOL PAPER OR THIN CARDBOARD

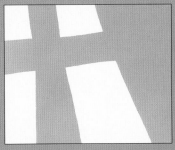

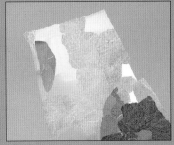

1. Make a rough plan for your collage on a piece of scrap paper. Mark on the position of roads, a park, buildings, cars, and so on.

2. On a large piece of paper or cardboard, paint the shapes which are the roads on your plan, with acrylic or poster paint.

3. For the park, rip pieces of light-colored paper from old magazines and glue them. Add green paper for grass.

4. Fill in the areas for the buildings with dark pieces of paper. Rip shapes for the buildings and add some windows.

5. For the cars, rip a shape for the body, with wheel arches ripped out. Glue two wheels behind and windows on top.

6. For a cat, rip the body from magazine paper which has a texture on it. Glue on paws. Cut out an eye and glue it on, too.

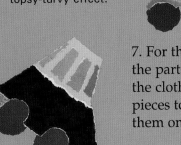

The shapes in this collage were glued on at different angles to give it a topsy-turvy effect.

7. For the people, rip all the parts of the body and the clothes. Glue the pieces together, then glue them onto the collage.

Wax resist fish and butterflies

BRISTOL PAPER

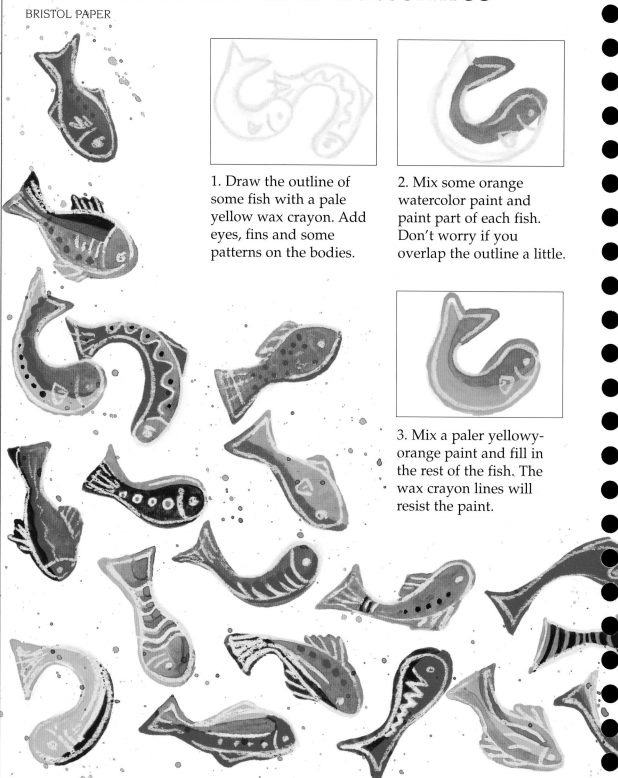

1. Draw the outline of some fish with a pale yellow wax crayon. Add eyes, fins and some patterns on the bodies.

2. Mix some orange watercolor paint and paint part of each fish. Don't worry if you overlap the outline a little.

3. Mix a paler yellowy-orange paint and fill in the rest of the fish. The wax crayon lines will resist the paint.

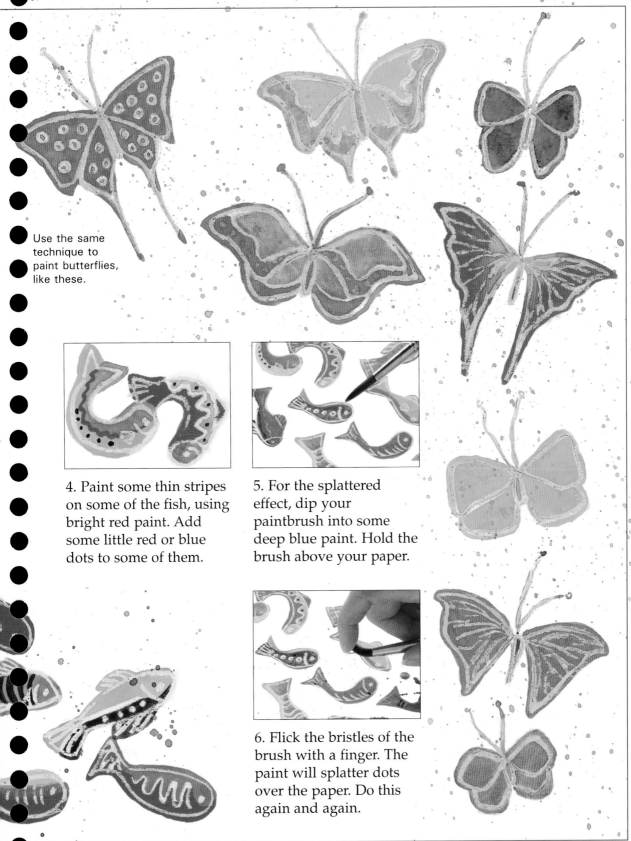

Use the same technique to paint butterflies, like these.

4. Paint some thin stripes on some of the fish, using bright red paint. Add some little red or blue dots to some of them.

5. For the splattered effect, dip your paintbrush into some deep blue paint. Hold the brush above your paper.

6. Flick the bristles of the brush with a finger. The paint will splatter dots over the paper. Do this again and again.

Cityscape

WHITE OR COLORED PAPER OR THIN CARDBOARD

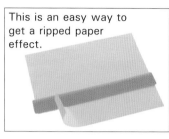

This is an easy way to get a ripped paper effect.

1. For the road, lay a ruler on a piece of paper. Press firmly on the ruler and rip the paper along its edge.

2. Glue the road along the bottom of a large piece of paper. Rip another piece, with an angle at one end, and glue it on.

3. For the buildings, rip rectangles from lots of different kinds of paper. Rip tower shapes on one end of some of them.

Use different types of paper, such as brown wrapping paper, or old envelopes.

4. Arrange the rectangles of paper along the road, then glue them on. Overlap some of them to get a 3-D effect.

5. Cut out and glue lots of windows on some of the buildings. Glue some strips of white tissue paper on some, too.

6. Draw an outline around a few of the buildings with a black felt-tip pen. Draw windows on some of them, too.

Draw some tiny cars. This helps to make the buildings look massive.

171

Sheep on a hill

THICK BRISTOL OR WATERCOLOR PAPER

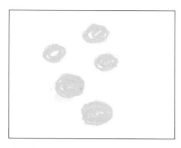

1. Use a white oil pastel to draw ovals for the sheep's bodies. They are shown here in yellow so that you can see them.

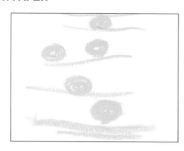

2. Use the pastel to draw some horizontal lines in front of the ovals. Add some thinner lines between the sheep, too.

3. Then, brush a rectangle of watery purple and pink watercolor paint on top. The pastel resists the paint.

4. Hold the paper and gently tilt it from side to side so that the colors blend together. Then, leave it to dry.

5. Mix some dark blue paint or ink and paint a little oval on each sheep's body for a head. Add four stick legs, too.

6. Dip your paintbrush into thick white paint and splatter the snow by following steps 5 and 6 on page 169.

Other ideas

Draw flowers with white and yellow oil pastels. Paint green watercolor on top, then scratch the stalks with a craft knife.

Draw trees, grass and clouds in white. Paint over the sky, trees and grass. When the paint's dry, scratch across the pastel.

Draw buildings with oil pastels. Add white roads and hills. Paint over them with blue, then sponge thick white paint on top.

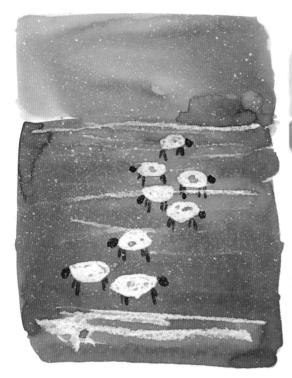

The cloud effect in the sky happens when you tilt the paper and the colors blend together.

The tufts of grass were painted in a slightly darker green once the background had dried.

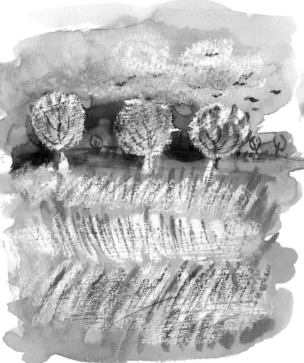

If you scratch the paint away with a craft knife, the pastel and paper are revealed underneath.

The windows were painted over the pastel, which resisted the paint, making uneven lines.

Techniques for feathers

Birds' feathers can be speckled or spotted, striped or plain. On this double page there are a few techniques for painting and drawing birds and feathers.

To do a feather, start by painting a simple feather shape, like this.

Look at real feathers to get some ideas.

These spots were printed with an eraser on the end of a pencil, dipped in white paint.

Use the tip of a fine brush to paint fine lines on a feather.

The speckles on this feather were drawn first with oil pastels, then watercolor was painted on top.

Draw a feather with a soft 6B pencil, then add stripes with ink.

The stripes on the feather below were added while the ink was still wet.

Use chalk pastels to draw a soft, downy feather.

Pheasant

1. Paint the body using watery brown watercolor paint. Go over the head, tail, tummy and legs with a darker brown.

2. While the paint is wet, add black and brown dots to the tail and tummy. Paint dark areas on the head, beak and neck.

3. Paint around the eye with red paint. Use a thin felt-tip pen to outline the body, adding feathers to the wing and tail.

Spotted woodpecker

1. Paint a thick black line for the head, back and tail. Then use finer lines for the rest of the body.

2. Paint a line on the tummy with watery ink. Fingerpaint spots on the tail with acrylic paint.

3. Fill in the body with a peach-colored chalk pastel. Add markings on the back and wing.

4. Draw a red chalk patch on the head and tummy. Smudge the pastel a little with your finger.

This woodpecker was painted in ink. The branch was drawn with a 6B pencil.

Swimming turtles

WATERCOLOR PAPER

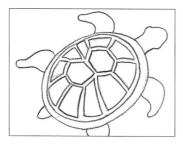

1. Use a blue pencil to draw a faint outline of a turtle's shell. Add a head, flippers, a tail and markings on the shell.

2. Paint markings on the shell with turquoise watercolor paint. Before the shapes dry, add a few dots. The paint will run.

3. Fill in the head, tail and flippers with turquoise paint. Then, add dots of paint to them before they have dried.

To get this effect around the turtle, the painting was covered with plastic foodwrap.

This is the effect you get when salt crystals are sprinkled onto the wet paint.

4. Paint the paper around the turtle with clean water. While the paper is still wet, add patches of green and turquoise paint.

5. Either sprinkle salt crystals over the wet paint, or lay a layer of plastic foodwrap over the painting. Leave it to dry.

6. Then, when the paint has dried completely, brush off all the salt crystals, or pull off the plastic foodwrap.

Pastel landscape

ANY TYPE OF YELLOW OR BEIGE PAPER

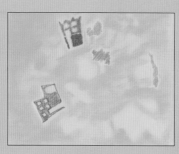

1. Using a pencil, draw a plan for your pastel landscape on a large piece of yellow or beige colored paper.

2. Make the pencil lighter with an eraser. Then, fill in the background with a mustard-colored chalk pastel. Fill in some shapes.

3. Draw a tree trunk with a brown pastel. Add green leaves, then add shadows and highlights with dark and light green pastels.

4. For the buildings, fill in the main part with chalk pastels, leaving gaps for the window frames and door, then fill them in.

5. Draw green stems and leaves for the sunflowers. Add darker lines. Use yellow for the flowers and add orange on top.

6. Draw a white oval for the fountain. Outline the boy and the dog in blue, then fill them in. Fill in the water last of all.

7. Use the mustard chalk pastel to go over parts of the background again, around each of the things you have drawn.

To stop pastels from smudging, you can fix them with fixative spray or hair spray.

Cloud people

WATERCOLOR PAPER

Wipe the brush on a paper towel after each shape.

1. Mix some watery dark blue watercolor paint, then use a thick brush to paint a large patch of color, like this.

2. Brush some of the paint away from the patch to make the shapes for the clown's hat and collar. Let the patch dry a little.

3. Then, using a clean, dry brush, lift off a curve of paint for the clown's chin and shapes for the nose and eyebrows.

4. Leave the paint to dry completely, then use dark blue paint to add shadows under the nose and chin.

5. Add lines for the eyebrows and the eyes. Then, paint a line for the side of the face and some curved lines on the collar.

This character is an admiral with a long nose, a curly moustache and a beard. Lines and dots show his uniform.

Add a crown and hair ribbons to create a princess.

You can lift off paint to make the brim of a hat or a bulbous nose.

6. Use a thin brush and the dark blue paint to paint the outline of the hat. Add two small circles for bells.

7. Paint pupils in each eye. Then, add a little line above and below each eye, for the clown's face paint.

8. Paint two lines for the lips. Add little lines at each side of the mouth, to make the clown look as if it is grinning.

9. Paint two curved lines at the side of the face for the ears. Then, add several curved lines for ruffles on the collar.

Scratched patterns

BRISTOL PAPER

This patch was scratched with random shapes and patterns.

1. Use different oil pastels to draw patches of color on a piece of Bristol paper. Make sure that the patches join together.

2. Mix a little water with black acrylic paint, but don't make it too thin. Cover the oil pastel completely with the paint.

3. Leave the paint until it is almost dry. Then, use a screwdriver to scratch lines, revealing the pastel underneath.

4. Scratch several more lines down the paint, then scratch lines across to make a large grid. Scratch a border, too.

5. Draw a simple outline of a bird in part of the grid. Add curved lines for feathers, a wing, an eye and a beak.

6. If you make a mistake, paint some of the black acrylic paint on top and let it dry a little before scratching it again.

Giraffe collage

A LARGE PIECE OF THIN CARDBOARD

  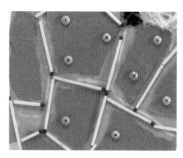

Don't glue these areas yet.

1. Glue a piece of brown butcher paper onto some cardboard. Then, rip another piece of paper. Glue it across the bottom.

2. Cut out a giraffe's body and legs. Cut a head from corrugated cardboard. Glue the pieces to the background, like this.

3. Rip lots of patches from brown paper and glue them onto the body. Glue matchsticks around them. Add beads or dried beans.

4. Glue fluffy feathers or lots of pieces of yarn down the neck for the mane. Glue long feathers over the top.

5. Wrap black yarn around each hoof and glue on things like matchsticks, feathers and pieces of shiny paper.

6. For the giraffe's antlers, twist the wire off an old clothespin. Glue a large, dried seed or bean onto the end of each pin.

Make birds to glue around the giraffe by ripping a paper body and wing. Join them with a paper fastener.

7. For eyes, glue together things such as feathers, dried plants and buttons. Glue them on, then glue the rest of the body down.

Don't worry if you don't have exactly the objects shown on this picture - use whatever you can find.

The tail was tucked underneath the body before the body was glued down.

Pencil bugs

ANY PAPER WITH A SMOOTH SURFACE

1. Use a pencil with a soft lead (a 6B pencil is ideal) to draw a simple outline of an insect on your paper.

2. Shade the insect's body, making it darker close to the edges. Fill in the head and legs. Add any spots or patterns, too.

3. Rub lines across your drawing with an eraser to smudge the pencil a little. Rub the lines in different directions.

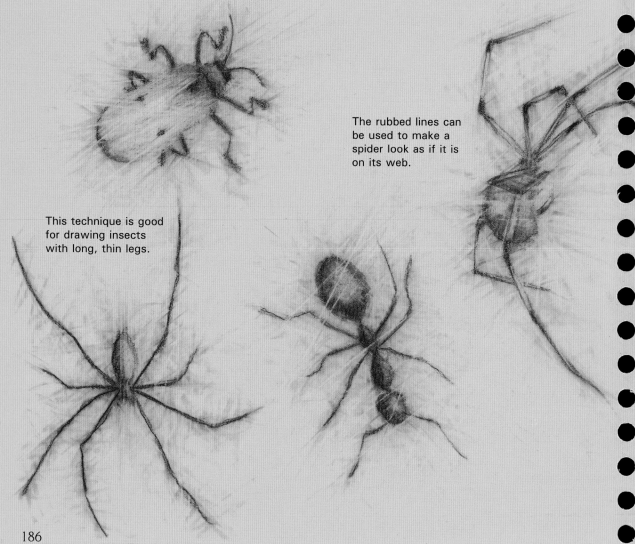

The rubbed lines can be used to make a spider look as if it is on its web.

This technique is good for drawing insects with long, thin legs.

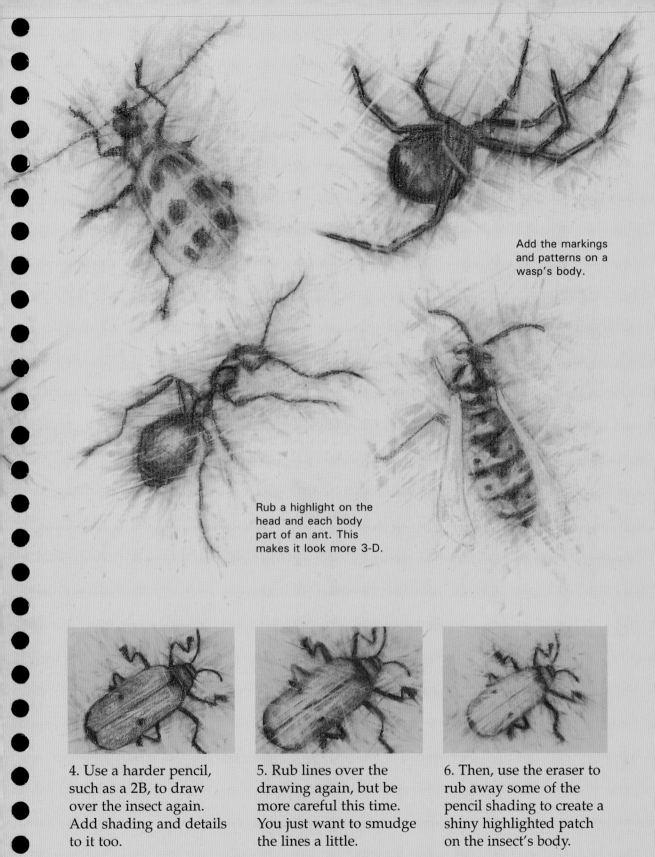

Add the markings and patterns on a wasp's body.

Rub a highlight on the head and each body part of an ant. This makes it look more 3-D.

4. Use a harder pencil, such as a 2B, to draw over the insect again. Add shading and details to it too.

5. Rub lines over the drawing again, but be more careful this time. You just want to smudge the lines a little.

6. Then, use the eraser to rub away some of the pencil shading to create a shiny highlighted patch on the insect's body.

More ideas

Over the next four pages there are lots more ideas for using the techniques in this book. Turn back to the pages which are mentioned to find out how they were done.

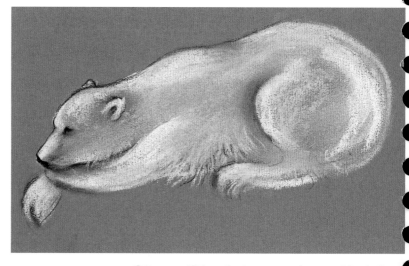

This polar bear was drawn with chalk pastels, like the leopard on page 161.

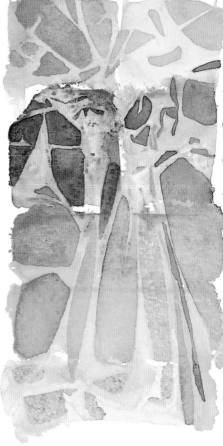

These birds were made with ripped paper from old magazines (see pages 166-167).

This pattern was created with plastic foodwrap (see pages 138-139).

These buildings were based on the domed ones on pages 154-155.

This is another idea for using the wet- on-wet technique (see pages 164-165).

These insects use the same technique as the fish on pages 168-169.

This dog was painted with inks and chalk pastels (see pages 150-151).

189

This lady was outlined using one continuous line (see pages 158-159).

Loose outlines can make pictures like this dog look animated.

These textured houses are different styles and colors from the ones on pages 126-127.

Different leaves have been added to these blow-painted trees (see pages 152-153).

This colorful picture is a variation of the doodle painting on page 136.

The background for this frog was created using plastic foodwrap (see pages 176-177).

The background for this Western sunset was created by dragging paint with pieces of cardboard (see page 108).

To make a snail collage, rip pieces of tissue paper (see pages 142-143).

Details on this painted giraffe were added with pastels (see page 161) and pen.

191

Shading effects

You can create different types of shading by filling in shapes with different patterns or marks. Experiment with some of the ideas here to fill in your own drawings.

Draw lots of parallel lines next to each other, like on the bird's beak. This is called hatching.

Draw lots of lines at one angle, then do more lines across them. This is called cross hatching.

The strength of shading depends on the distance between the hatched lines.

Cross hatching

Fill a shape with lots of dots. If you draw them close together the shading will look darker.

Shading with dots is called stippling.

Fill a shape with lots of spirals. They are good to show curly hair or fur.

ART
projects

These beetles were drawn
using the pastel and ink
technique on pages 272-273.

Materials

These two pages show the variety of art materials that are used in the projects that follow.

Paper ideas

Below are some of the different papers that are used for the projects. Beneath the heading on most of the pages you'll find a suggestion for the kind of paper to use for that project.

Using a craft knife

Some of the projects suggest using a craft knife to cut out shapes. When you use one, always put a pile of old magazines or one or two pieces of thick cardboard under the paper you are cutting.

Be very careful when you use a craft knife. Keep your fingers away from the blade.

This pink paper has been textured with paint (see pages 212-213).

Patterned wrapping paper

Pages ripped from old magazines

Tissue paper

Corrugated cardboard from an old box. Rip off the top layer of paper to reveal the bumpy surface.

Colored corrugated cardboard from an art supply store

Paper with a raised texture

Art paper is thick and is usually sold in individual sheets.

Scraps of shiny paper from packaging or wrapping paper

Sequins

Thread

Threads and sequins are used on pages 224-227 and 248-249.

Ribbons

Chalk pastels

Bits and pieces

Some of the projects use things or items that you may have lying around your home. You'll find ideas for printing with erasers on pages 144, 198 and 234, and collages using found objects on pages 184 and 274.

Eraser

Found objects such as washers, press studs and paper fasteners.

Pastels and crayons

There are several projects that use pastels and wax crayons. You can usually buy them in sets.

Wax crayons

Paints, inks and pens

A variety of different paints are used in the projects. You will be told what type to use in the step-by-step instructions.

Mix watercolor paints with water before you use them.

Acrylic or poster paints can be used straight from their tube or container.

Several projects use a dip pen. If you don't have one, use a fountain pen instead.

Use colored ink with a dip pen.

Felt-tip pens

Printed people

BROWN WRAPPING PAPER OR COLORED ART PAPER

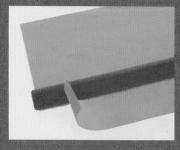

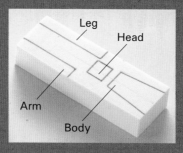

1. Lay a ruler on some brown wrapping paper or art paper. Then, rip off a strip of the paper, about 2¾ inches wide.

2. Use a ballpoint pen to draw these body parts on a rectangular eraser. Then, use a craft knife to cut out the pieces.

3. Put black acrylic paint or poster paint onto a kitchen sponge cloth. Spread it a little with the back of an old spoon.

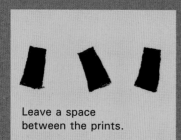

Leave a space between the prints.

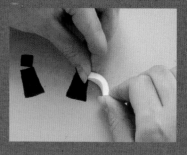

4. Press the body into the paint and press it onto the paper. Print more bodies, pressing the eraser into the paint each time.

5. Press the head into the paint, then print a head above each of the body shapes. Print each one at a slight angle.

6. To print the arms, dip the piece for the arm into the paint, then bend it a little before you press it onto the paper.

7. Print an arm on each side of the body, bending them each time so that each person is in a different position.

8. Print two legs onto each body in the same way as the arms. Bend the eraser as you print each leg, too.

9. When the paint has dried, use a black felt-tip pen to add hair, fingers and thumbs. You could add shoes, too.

To make a picture like this, print lots of strips of paper and glue them next to each other.

This row of people had feet added.

Tissue paper windows

TISSUE PAPER

1. Rip about fifteen strips of bright tissue paper. Make some of them the same length and width.

2. Using a glue stick, glue the edge of one of the strips. Then, press another strip onto the glue.

Tape the tissue paper to a window to get the full effect.

3. Continue gluing and overlapping different strips until you've made a rectangle.

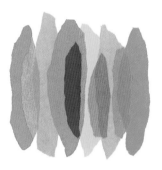

4. Glue some smaller contrasting strips on top. Make them overlap the edges of the long strips.

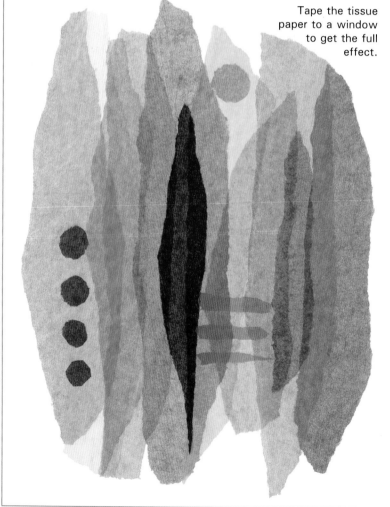

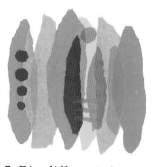

5. Rip different sizes of spots and glue them on. Glue on some little horizontal strips, too.

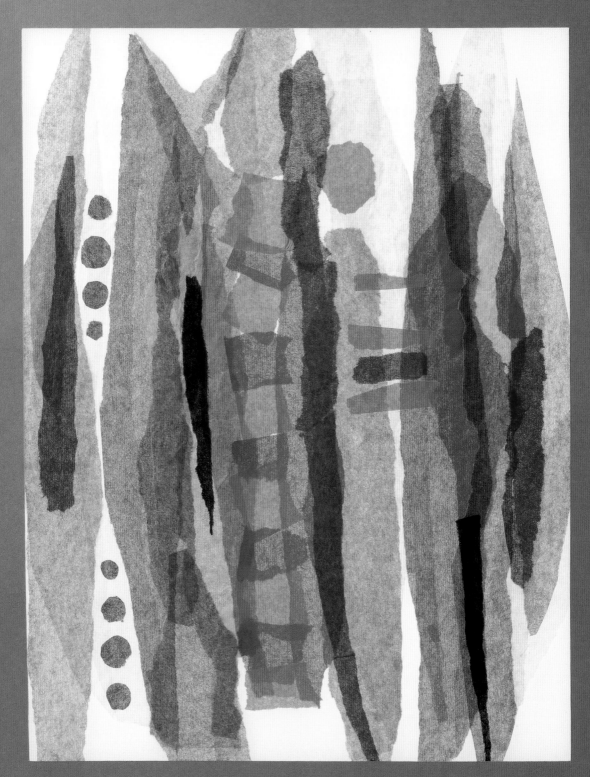

Glue the ends of the strips to the back of a simple frame (see page 257) and lean it against a window.

Paper mosaic cans

WHITE PAPER, LONG ENOUGH TO WRAP AROUND A CAN

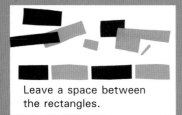

Leave a space between the rectangles.

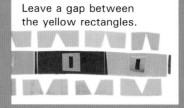

Leave a gap between the yellow rectangles.

1. Cut a rectangle of white paper the same height as a can*. Cut pieces of green paper and glue them along the middle of the paper.

2. Glue thin strips of red paper between the rectangles. Glue purple strips onto yellow squares, then glue them on top.

3. Cut rectangles from yellow paper, then cut a 'V' shape in each one. Glue them in a line on either side of the green strip.

All the paper used on these mosaic cans came from magazine pages.

You could use this technique to make a bookmark.

* Don't use cans that have been opened with a can
202 opener, as these leave jagged edges that can cut you.

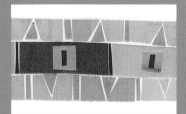

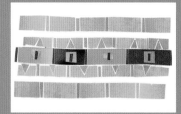

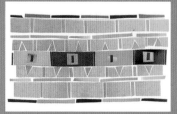

4. Cut triangles and thin strips from another shade of green paper and glue them in the spaces in the yellow rectangles.

5. Add two more lines of yellow rectangles and green strips. This time, leave a slightly wider space between the lines.

6. Glue thin yellow and green strips of paper in the spaces you left. Then, add green and red strips at the top and bottom.

These cans are ideal to use as a container for pens and pencils.

7. Cut a piece of book covering film large enough to cover the mosaic. Peel off the backing paper and smooth it on.

8. Wrap the paper around the can and trim the ends so that it fits exactly. Tape the ends together to secure them.

Spotted frogs

BRISTOL PAPER OR WATERCOLOR PAPER

1. Use green watercolor paint to paint a pear-shaped body on a piece of Bristol paper or watercolor paper.

2. Paint the frog's front and back legs coming out from the body. Make the back legs slightly longer than the front legs.

3. Paint three curved lines for the feet. Add three little dots at the end of each line for the frog's sticky pads.

Use this technique to decorate other simple shapes, like these snakes.

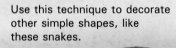

4. Paint lots more frogs to fill your paper. Paint them close together and facing in different directions, like this.

5. When the paint is dry, pour some lemon juice onto a saucer. Paint dots of juice all over a frog. Make them different sizes.

6. Then, use a scrunched-up tissue to dab off the juice. It will lift off some of the paint, leaving brightly colored dots.

204

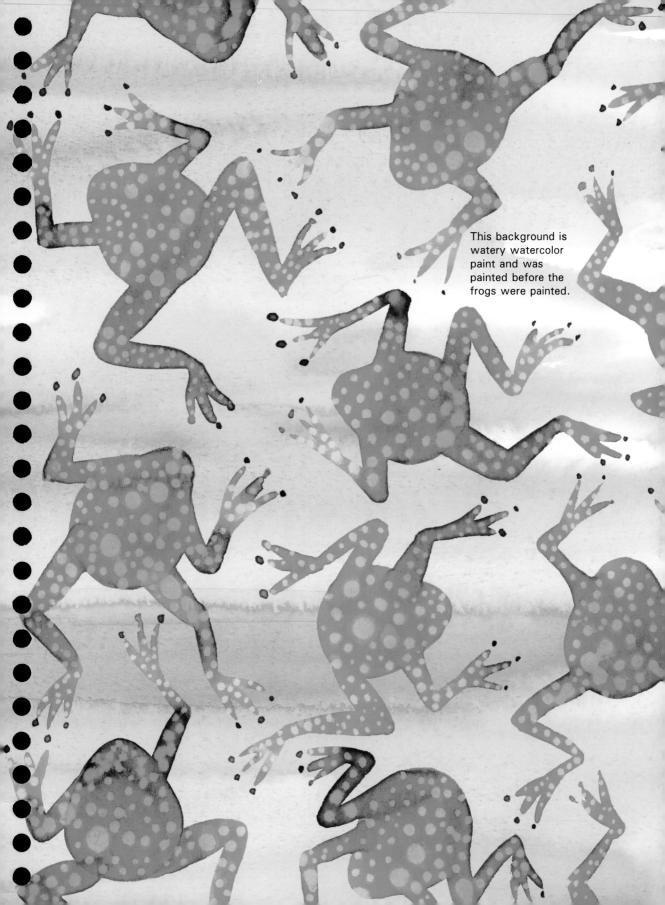

This background is watery watercolor paint and was painted before the frogs were painted.

Punched holes

COLORED PAPER OR TEXTURED PAPER (SEE PAGES 212-213)

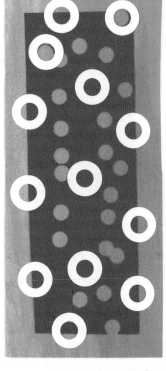

1. Cut a rectangle from colored or textured paper. The sides don't have to be exactly the same length.

2. Cut two strips from a contrasting color of paper. Then, use a hole puncher to punch a row of holes along them.

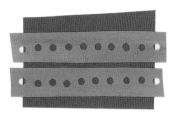

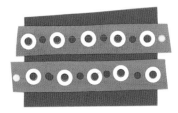

3. Lay the strips on some newspaper and spread glue on the back of each one. Then, press them onto the rectangle.

4. Press a reinforcement ring around alternate holes along the strips, to create a pattern of rings and punched holes.

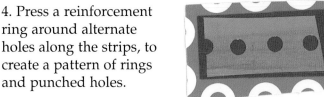

Experiment with different patterns of rings and where you punch holes in the paper.

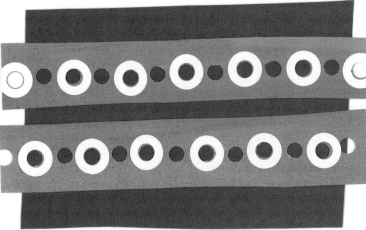

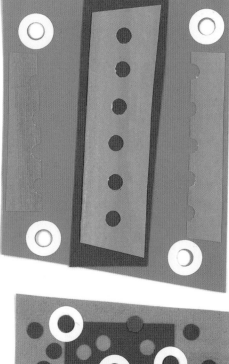

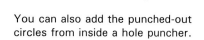

The instructions below show you how to make this kind of pattern.

You can also add the punched-out circles from inside a hole puncher.

1. To make the example above, cut a rectangle of blue paper. Then, cut another, slightly smaller, purple rectangle.

Use a craft knife.

2. Press reinforcement rings onto the purple rectangle. Then, cut a small rectangle out of the middle of the paper, through the rings.

Glue the small rectangle in the middle.

3. Trim a little piece off each side of the small rectangle. Then, glue the pieces of purple paper onto the blue paper.

Wacky faces

CORRUGATED CARDBOARD AND COLORED PAPER

1. Draw a simple outline of a face on a piece of scrap paper. Draw a line down the middle with a shape for a nose, like this.

2. Trace your drawing onto tracing paper. Then, turn the tracing over and scribble over the lines with your pencil.

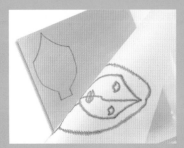

3. Turn the tracing over, then use a ballpoint pen to draw over the outline of the face onto some pale paper. Cut it out.

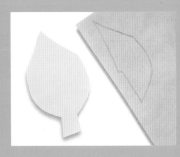

4. Lay the tracing onto some darker paper. Draw over the outline of the right-hand side of the face only and cut it out.

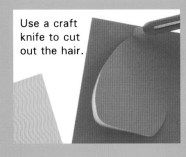

Use a craft knife to cut out the hair.

5. Trace the hair onto thin cardboard and cut it out. Place some corrugated cardboard behind the hole and secure it with tape.

6. Glue the face onto the hair. Then, glue on the right side of the face. Cut out, and glue on, lips and eyes. Draw on eyelashes.

7. Cut out a sweater from another piece of cardboard and glue it on top so that it overlaps the hair and neck.

Male face

1. Follow steps 1 to 4. Then, trace the whole outline onto cardboard and cut it out. Tape black cardboard behind.

2. Glue the right side onto the face, then use a craft knife to cut the eyes. Glue the face onto the corrugated cardboard.

This girl's sweater was cut out of the background.

This corrugated cardboard was bought in an art supply store.

Ink blocks and spots

WATERCOLOR PAPER

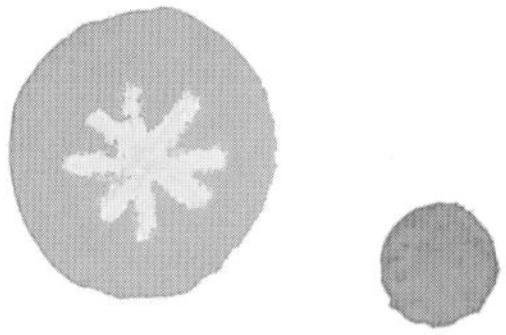

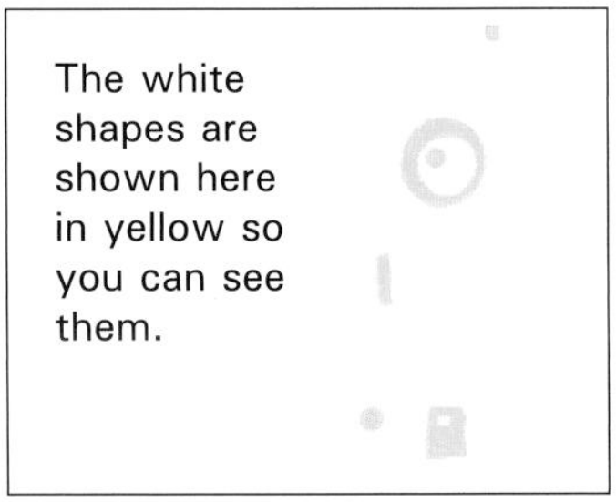

The white shapes are shown here in yellow so you can see them.

1. Use a white and a lime green wax crayon to draw a pattern of dots, circles and rectangles on watercolor paper.

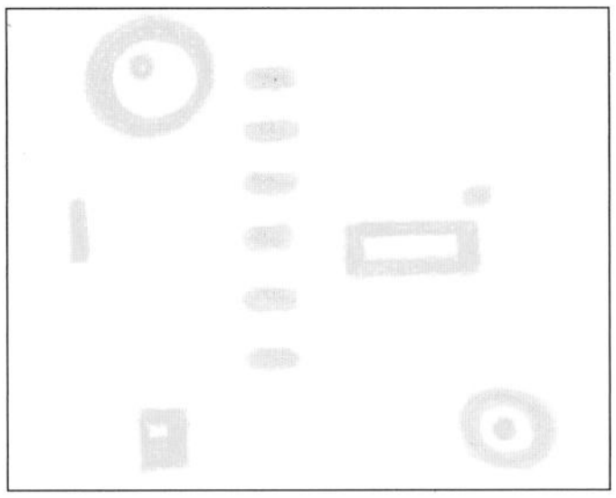

2. Add a row of green lines beside them, then draw more crayon shapes. Don't make them too close together.

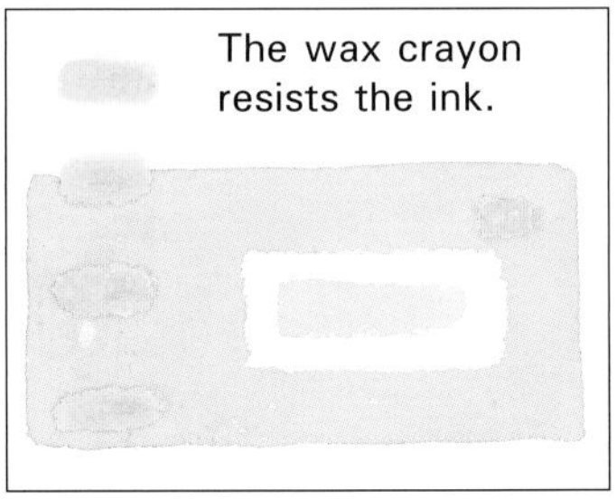

The wax crayon resists the ink.

3. Mix water with some turquoise ink and paint rectangles and squares over some of the shapes. Let the ink dry.

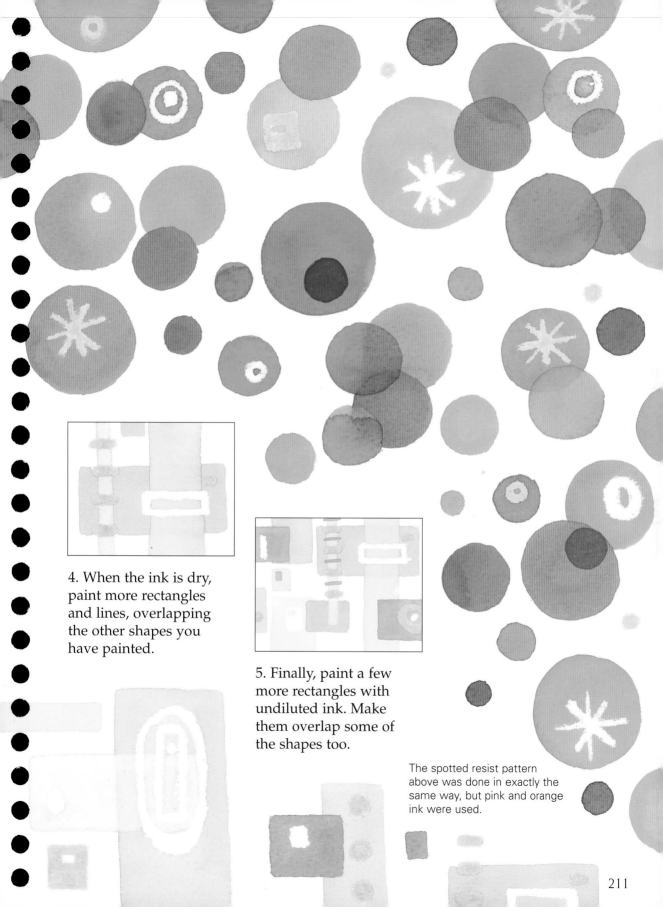

4. When the ink is dry, paint more rectangles and lines, overlapping the other shapes you have painted.

5. Finally, paint a few more rectangles with undiluted ink. Make them overlap some of the shapes too.

The spotted resist pattern above was done in exactly the same way, but pink and orange ink were used.

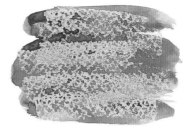

Texturing paper

Several of the projects in this book, including the 3-D bugs on pages 220-221 and the paper weaving on pages 242-243, use pieces of paper that have been textured by using different paint techniques.

Experiment with the examples on the following four pages to create your own papers.

Wax resist

1. Rub the side of a wax crayon or oil pastel over a piece of slightly textured paper. Press hard on the crayon as you rub.

2. Mix some water with paint and brush it over the paper. The wax will resist the paint, leaving the texture of the paper.

Brushmarks

1. Dip a thick household paintbrush in yellow paint, then brush it in stripes across a piece of white paper.

2. Mix some red with the yellow to make orange. Brush it lightly across the yellow paint so that you leave brushmarks.

3. While the paint is still wet, brush red paint on top of the yellow and orange paint, leaving marks as before.

These samples of paper have been textured using the techniques shown above.

Swirly circles

1. Dip a dry, broad paintbrush into thick acrylic paint so that the paint just covers the tips of the bristles.

2. Brush the paint around and around on a piece of paper, pressing hard. You should get lots of individual brushmarks.

3. Dip the tips of the bristles into the paint again and brush another circle beside the first one. Do this again and again.

Sponge marks

1. Dip a piece of sponge into some paint, then dab it onto a piece of paper. Dip it into the paint each time you dab it on.

2. Then, dab a darker shade of paint over the top of it, leaving some of the original color showing through.

3. You can even sponge a third color on top, or dab on some gold or silver acrylic paint, if you have some.

The sample of paper below has been textured by sponging blue paint onto white paper.

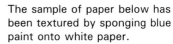

Textured paper picture

BLACK PAPER AND SMALL PIECES OF WHITE PAPER

The steps on this page show you different ways of making textured paper and patterns with paint, pastels and collage. You don't need to follow the ideas exactly, just experiment with the different techniques. You could then cut your samples into squares and then glue them together to make a picture.

1. Follow the steps on page 213 to paint a swirly circle with light blue or ultramarine paint. Use a thick paintbrush.

2. Paint another piece of paper with blue paint. When it's dry, cut it into strips and glue them onto a piece of white paper.

3. Use a chalk pastel or oil pastel to scribble thick lines across a piece of paper. Do it quickly and don't try to be too neat.

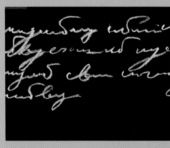

4. Use a white chalk pastel to write long lines of flowing, joined-up writing across a piece of black paper.

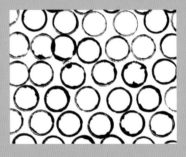

5. Spread black paint on an old saucer, then dip a bottle top into it. Use the bottle top to print several rows of circles.

6. Paint two blue lines across some paper. Glue on two strips that have been painted with black paint. Add a pink square.

7. Use paint to fill in blocks of blue on a piece of paper. Use a chalk pastel to draw a white line across the middle.

8. Cut the pieces of textured paper into rough squares. Arrange them on a large piece of black paper, then glue them on.

Dangling bread shapes

SLICED BREAD

1. Press a cookie cutter firmly into a slice of bread. Then, push the shape out of the cutter. Cut lots more shapes.

2. Press the end of a straw into each shape to make a hole for hanging it up. Use a fat straw, if you have one.

To make a hanging chain like this one, make two holes with the straw. Tie the shapes together with thread.

3. Lift the shapes onto a baking rack and leave them overnight. By the morning they will be dry and hard.

4. Mix some white paint with household glue and paint it around the edge of each shape. Then, paint one side.

5. When the paint is dry, paint the other side. When the paint is completely dry, use a pencil to draw on simple patterns.

216

6. Fill in the patterns with different colors of acrylic paint. Paint the edge of the shapes when the pattern has dried.

7. To hang the shapes, push a long piece of thread through each hole made by the straw and tie a knot.

217

Folded dyed paper

WHITE OR LIGHT-COLORED TISSUE PAPER

1. Fold a rectangle of tissue paper about the size of this page in half. Then, fold it in half three more times.

2. Dip a paintbrush in clean water and paint it all over the folded paper. Do this again and again until the paper is damp.

3. Paint a band of blue ink across the middle of the paper. Do this two or three times so that the ink soaks into the paper.

The paper below had blobs of ink painted all over it when it was folded.

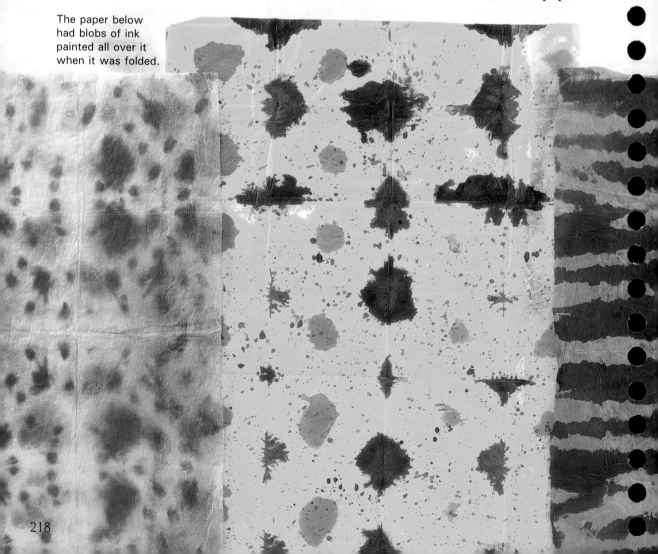

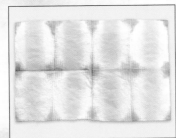

4. Paint each corner of the folded paper with purple ink. Let the ink soak into the paper and mix with the blue ink.

5. Leave the folded paper to dry. When it is completely dry, unfold it very carefully to reveal the dyed pattern.

6. Dip a paintbrush into purple ink. Hold it above the paper and flick the bristles of the brush to splatter the ink all over.

This green paper had lots of stripes painted across it.

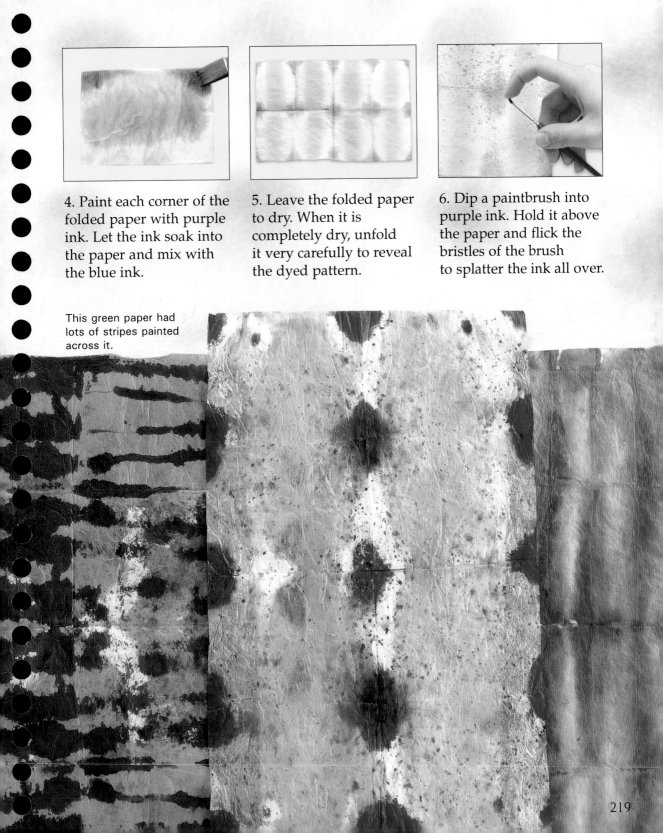

3-D bugs

TEXTURED PAPERS (SEE PAGES 212-213)

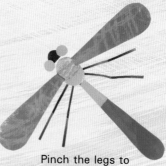

Pinch the legs to
make them bend.

1. Cut out the middle and lower parts of a bug's body from textured paper. Glue the pieces onto some thick paper or cardboard.

2. Cut out a dome-shaped head and two eyes, and glue them on. Also cut out and glue on yellow shapes to fit on the body.

3. Cut out and glue on two lower wings. Cut four legs. Glue on the ends closest to the body. Pinch them in the middle.

The bug below is the one described in the steps.

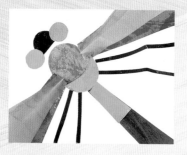

Pull the folded ends out to make it stand up.

4. Cut out two upper wings from tracing paper or tissue paper. Pinch each narrow end to make a fold. Glue on that end only.

5. For the ridges down the body, cut a strip of paper. Fold each end inward, then fold the ends back on themselves.

This orange bug has three sets of wings cut from textured paper.

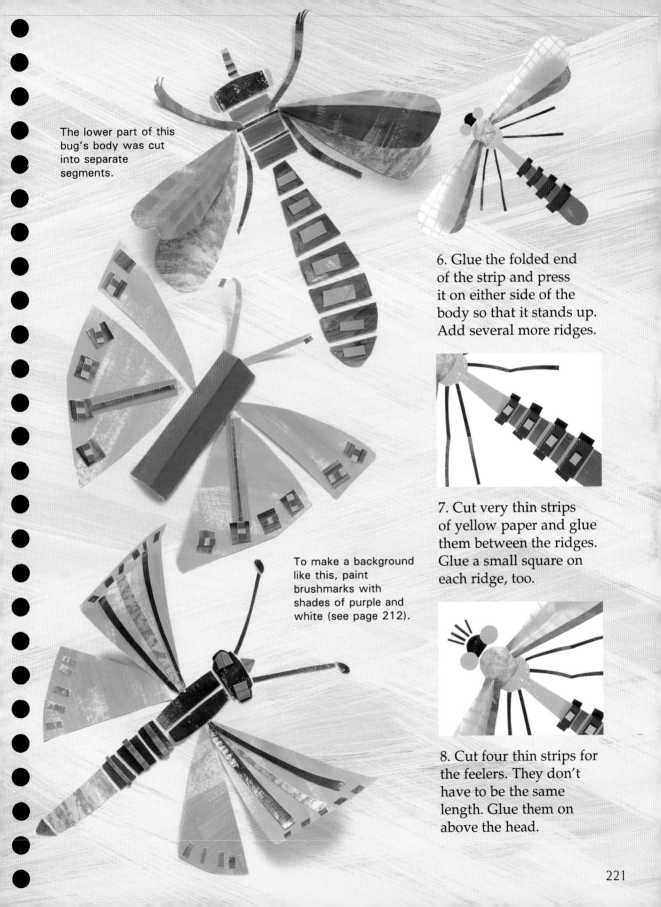

The lower part of this bug's body was cut into separate segments.

6. Glue the folded end of the strip and press it on either side of the body so that it stands up. Add several more ridges.

7. Cut very thin strips of yellow paper and glue them between the ridges. Glue a small square on each ridge, too.

To make a background like this, paint brushmarks with shades of purple and white (see page 212).

8. Cut four thin strips for the feelers. They don't have to be the same length. Glue them on above the head.

221

Busy street collage

OLD MAGAZINES AND COLORED PAPER

1. Cut lots of different textures from magazines. Cut pieces of hair, ears and lips from photos of people, too.

2. Draw a hairstyle on a piece of paper with hair texture and cut it out. Glue it onto a small piece of white paper.

3. Lay tracing paper over the hair and draw a face and neck to fit it. Turn the tracing over and rub pencil over the lines.

To make a street scene, use the ideas shown here to make lots of figures. Glue them onto a background.

Instead of a wall, you could cut out textures of plants and glue them on to make a hedge.

Press firmly.

Add other details, like a teddy bear.

4. Turn the tracing back over. Lay it on top of some paper with a skin tone. Draw over the face again, then cut it out.

5. Glue the face on the hair. Cut out a mouth and ear, then draw eyes and a nose. Cut a dress from textured paper and glue it on.

6. Cut out legs, arms and a pair of shoes and glue them on. Add a sleeve at the top of the arm and a heart-shaped pocket.

Simple stitches

Stitches can be used to decorate not only material, but paper and cardboard too. These pages show you how to do some simple stitches and how to tie a knot to secure the thread before you start to stitch.

Tying a knot

Hold your nail tightly against your thumb as you pull.

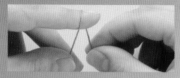 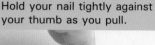 

1. Hold the end of a piece of thread between your thumb and first finger. Wrap the thread around your finger once.

2. Rub your finger hard along your thumb. You should feel the thread rolling and twisting between them.

3. Put your middle fingernail at the top of the rolled thread. Pull the long end of the thread hard and make a knot.

Running (or basting) stitch

1. Thread a needle, then make a knot in one end. Push your needle up through the paper and pull the thread through.

2. Push the point of the needle down through the paper, a little way away. Then, pull the needle through from the back.

3. Push the needle up again a little way from your first stitch, then push it down again, pulling the thread tight.

 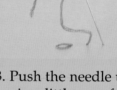

4. Continue pushing the needle upward and downward in the same way, so that you make a line of stitches.

5. To finish off, stitch through the last stitch you made and pull the thread tight. Then, stitch through it again.

6. Push your needle through these stitches again, two more times. Then, cut the thread a little way away from the knot.

 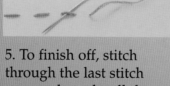

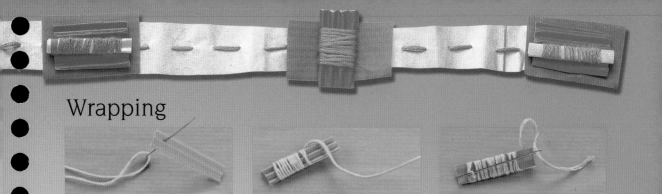

Wrapping

1. Cut a thin strip of cardboard or fabric. Thread a needle, then push it up through the strip, from the back.

2. Wrap the thread around and around the strip so that you cover a section of it. Pull the thread tight as you wrap.

3. When you have wrapped enough, stitch through the knot on the back two or three times to finish off.

Couching

1. Cut a piece of thick thread and lay it where you want to stitch it. Push your needle up from the back, next to the thread.

2. Push the needle down on the other side of the thread to make a small straight stitch. This will secure the thick thread.

3. Continue making small stitches over the thicker thread along its length. Finish off on the back with one or two stitches.

This is the back.

Sewing on a sequin and a bead

You will need to use a fine needle for this.

1. Push your needle up through the paper or fabric, but don't pull it all the way through. Slide a sequin onto the needle.

2. Slide a bead on top and pull the thread through both of them. Then, push the needle back through the hole in the sequin.

3. Pull the needle all the way through to the back of the paper or fabric. Then, tie a knot with the two ends of the thread.

Stitched paper squares

CORRUGATED CARDBOARD AND TEXTURED PAPER

Don't glue the small rectangles on.

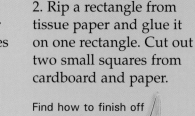

1. Cut 16 rectangles of corrugated cardboard or textured paper (see pages 212-213). Make them roughly the same size.

2. Rip a rectangle from tissue paper and glue it on one rectangle. Cut out two small squares from cardboard and paper.

3. Thread a needle and make a knot in the end. Holding all the pieces in place, stitch a bead in the middle of the squares.

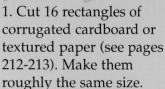

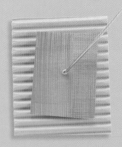

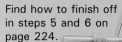
Find how to finish off in steps 5 and 6 on page 224.

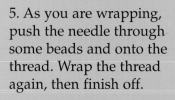

4. Then, stitch up through a rectangle of cardboard and one of textured paper. Wrap the thread around them several times.

5. As you are wrapping, push the needle through some beads and onto the thread. Wrap the thread again, then finish off.

6. On another rectangle, lay three pieces of thick thread. Use couching stitches (see page 225) to hold them down.

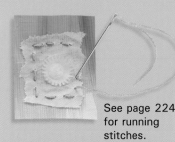
See page 224 for running stitches.

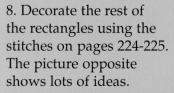

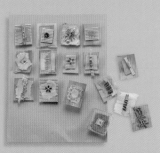

7. Lay a sequin on another rectangle, then put a piece of tissue paper on top. Use running stitches to stitch around the sequin.

8. Decorate the rest of the rectangles using the stitches on pages 224-225. The picture opposite shows lots of ideas.

9. When all the rectangles are decorated, use strong glue to stick them in rows on a large piece of thick paper.

Foil fish

WATERCOLOR PAPER

The drops of water and the salt make the ink spread.

1. For the sea, mix turquoise ink with water, then use a thick brush to paint it all over a piece of watercolor paper.

2. Use the tip of the brush to dab on undiluted ink, then drop blobs of water onto it. Sprinkle salt all over, then let it dry.

3. For the sky, mix even more water with the turquoise ink and paint it all over another piece of watercolor paper.

4. While the sky is still wet, dab on darker ink in a few places. Then, dab it with a tissue to lift off some of the ink.

5. While the backgrounds are drying, draw a simple fish shape on a piece of kitchen foil. Tape it to a net vegetable bag.

6. Use your thumbnail to rub the foil, inside the outline of the fish. The pattern of the net will show on the foil.

Leave the foil taped to the net.

For the best effect, use felt-tip pens with permanent ink.

7. Fill in a stripe of green felt-tip pen along the back of the fish. Add a light green stripe under it, then fill in below with yellow.

8. Draw purple and orange lines on the head. Add an eye with a black pen. Cut out the fish, then make several more.

9. Brush the salt off the sea, then cut a wavy line across it. Glue the sea onto the sky, then add the fish on top.

The salt reacts with the ink to leave these watery patterns.

Fingerprinted farm animals

BROWN WRAPPING PAPER OR ANOTHER LIGHT COLORED PAPER

1. Dip your finger in black paint and fingerprint around and around for the body. Fingerprint the neck, head and ears, too.

2. Dip the edge of some cardboard into black paint, then scrape it sideways across the paper to print the legs. Fingerprint spots.

3. Print the eyes with white paint on the tip of your little finger. Draw the reins with an oil pastel or a chalk pastel.

Each of these horses had hooves printed with a small piece of cardboard.

4. Use a thin black felt-tip pen to outline the body, and draw the mane and tail. Outline the eyes and draw dots in them, too.

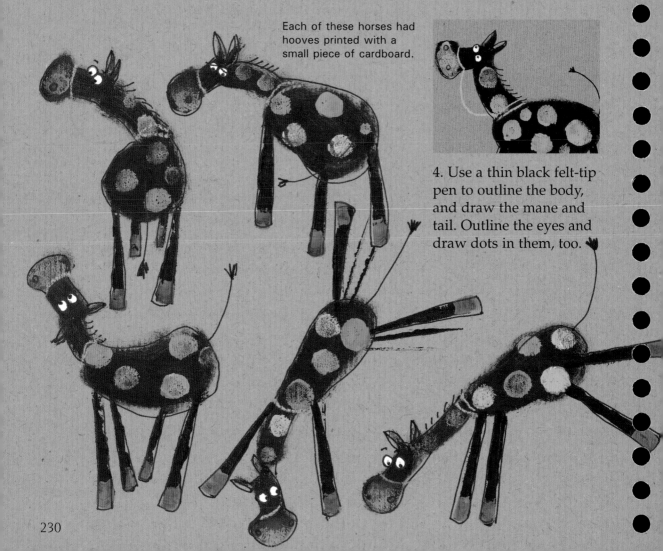

Chickens

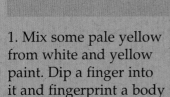

1. Mix some pale yellow from white and yellow paint. Dip a finger into it and fingerprint a body and a dot for the head.

2. Fingerprint a neck and three lines for the tail. Dip the tip of your little finger into white paint and print the eyes.

3. Scrape the edge of a piece of cardboard across the head to print a red beak and comb. Use it to print legs and feet, too.

4. When the paint is dry, outline the chicken with a black felt-tip pen. Draw around the eyes and add dots in them, too.

Print the horses with their head and legs in different positions.

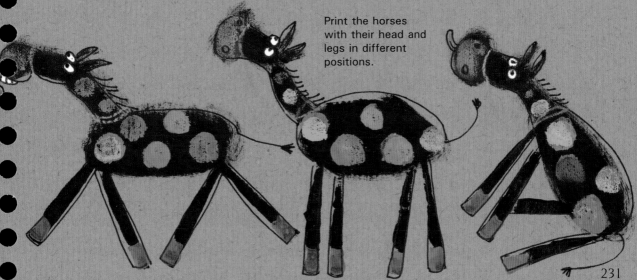

231

Collage cards

WRAPPING PAPER, CARDBOARD AND COLORED PAPERS

All these cards were made using the same technique. Some of them had extra shapes glued on top.

To make a row of triangles like this, cut 'v' shapes and fold them back.

1. Cut a rectangle of paper for the front of the card. Then, cut two smaller rectangles from paper or thin cardboard.

This makes the inside a different color from the front.

2. For the card itself, cut a rectangle of blue paper and fold it in half. Glue the largest rectangle on top and trim the edges.

3. Glue the smallest rectangle of paper onto the back of a piece of shiny paper or wrapping paper, then trim around it.

4. Then, use a craft knife to cut five lines that cross each other near the top of the paper. Push a pencil through the cuts.

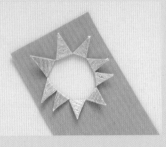

5. Gently fold each part back and crease them, so that the shiny paper makes a shape on the front of the paper.

6. Glue the pieces of paper onto the card. Then, use a gold pen to draw a pattern in the folded-back shape.

Shoe prints

WHITE OR A PALE COLOR OF PAPER

1. Use a ballpoint pen to draw the outline of a shoe on a rectangular eraser. Then, cut around it roughly with a craft knife.

2. Draw a buckle inside the shoe. Cut around the outline of the shoe carefully. Then, cut away the inside parts.

3. Spread some red acrylic or poster paint onto a kitchen sponge cloth. Then, press the flat side of the eraser into it.

4. Press the eraser onto a large piece of paper. Print it again and again on the paper, dipping it into the paint each time.

5. Cut out different shoes from more erasers (look at the page opposite for ideas). Print them between the red shoes.

6. When the paint is dry, draw around the prints with a thin felt-tip pen. Then, add little patterns with chalk or oil pastels.

You could use your printed paper to wrap presents.

The hats on the
paper above were
printed using exactly
the same technique.

Fun faces

THIN WHITE CARDBOARD OR BRISTOL PAPER

The hair on the face above was fingerprinted.

For dark shading on the neck, print the bubble wrap again with red paint.

The eyelashes on this face were printed with the edge of thin cardboard.

For a surprised look, print an open mouth with a bottle top.

1. Draw an outline of a face and neck. Then, rip small pieces of masking tape and press them around the outline.

Mix red and white paint if you don't have pink.

2. Spread some pink paint on a kitchen sponge cloth. Then, press the bumpy side of a piece of bubble wrap into the paint.

3. Press the bubble wrap down the side of the face and onto the neck. Rub the back of it to print the bubbly shapes.

4. Then, press a net vegetable bag onto the pink paint. Lay it on the other side of the face and rub your fingers over it.

5. Paint part of the rim of a plastic cup and use it to print the eyebrows and eyes. Paint the eyelashes with the end of a brush.

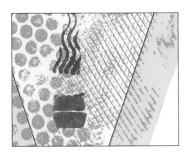

6. Print the nose with the ridged side of a corrugated cardboard triangle. Then, print the mouth with the end of an eraser.

Don't use too much paint when you paint the hair, so that you can see the brushmarks.

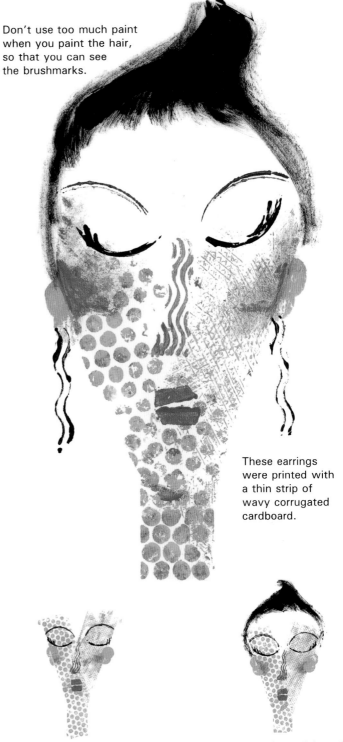

These earrings were printed with a thin strip of wavy corrugated cardboard.

7. Use a sponge to dab some paint onto the cheeks. Then, pull off the masking tape and print ears with a cork.

8. Dip an old toothbrush into black paint and use it to brush on the hair. Brush a little around the sides of the face, too.

237

Paper crocodile

COLORED ART PAPER

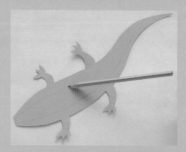

1. Draw a simple outline of a crocodile on thick paper and cut it out. Then, draw two wavy lines along its back.

2. Score along the lines by running a craft knife gently over the paper, without cutting all the way through.

3. Erase the pencil lines. Then, cut some teeth on either side of the wavy lines. Cut two large crosses for eyes.

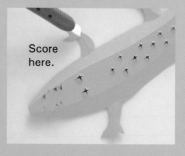

4. Turn it over and cut small crosses along the back, between the wavy lines. Score a curve where each leg meets the body.

5. Push a pencil gently into each cross. Use the pencil to push up the eyes and the teeth, too. Turn the crocodile over.

6. To shape the body, pinch along the wavy lines to crease them. Score along the legs and feet then crease them, too.

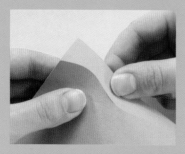

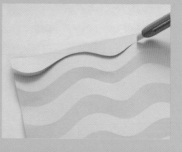

7. To make the water for the picture, score a wavy line along a piece of blue paper. Carefully crease along the scored line.

8. Turn the paper over and score another wavy line, following the shape of the first one. Then, crease this line.

9. Continue scoring and cutting lines on alternate sides of the paper. Then, cut a wavy line along the top of the paper.

Score the green paper on alternate sides.

10. For the background, score wavy lines on green paper. Then, cut a curve in some yellow paper and score a wavy line along it.

11. Cut long shapes for the grass at the bottom. Score and crease a curving line down the middle of each shape.

12. Arrange all the pieces. Then, put tiny dots of glue on the underside of each piece and glue them gently together.

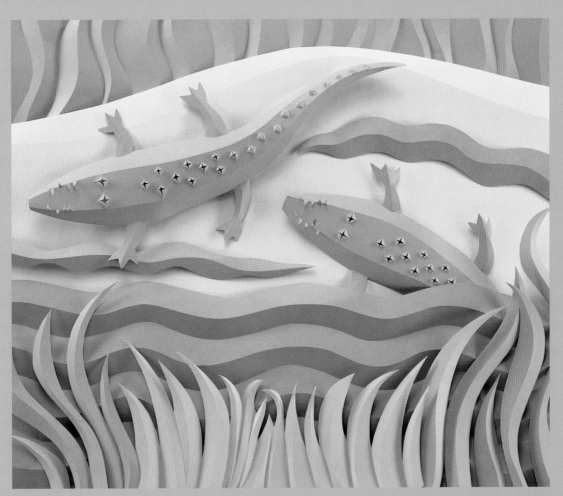

Paper weaving

ANY KIND OF COLORED PAPER

Make the slits a finger-width apart.

1. Draw a pencil line across one end of a rectangle of colored paper. Cut lots of slits up to the line.

2. Cut lots of strips of different colors of paper. Make them longer than the width of the rectangle in step 1.

Weave the strip over, then under.

3. Weave one strip of paper in and out of the slits in the rectangle. Then, push it up against the top of the slits.

4. Weave another strip below the first one. If the first strip started 'over' the cut strip, then the second starts 'under' it.

5. Continue weaving the strips until you have filled the rectangle. Push each strip against the one above it, as you go.

6. Turn your weaving over and use a piece of tape to secure the strips. Then, cut off the extra paper above the pencil line.

These two weavings used a mixture of wrapping paper and paper with a raised texture.

The weaving above used plastic from different grocery bags.

Try weaving pieces of ribbon and string between the paper strips.

You could cut a frame from cardboard (see page 256) and tape a paper weaving behind it.

This weaving had wavy slits cut in the rectangle, with straight strips woven through.

For a weaving like the one below, cut different widths of slits in the rectangle.

241

Woven hearts and stars

TEXTURED PAPER (SEE PAGES 212-213)

Don't cut all the way to the edges of the heart.

1. Cut a large heart from a piece of textured paper or thin cardboard. Then, cut slits down the heart with a craft knife.

2. Cut a strip of textured paper and weave it through the slits. Then, push it up toward the top of the heart.

3. Weave another strip below the first one. Make sure that you weave it over and under in the opposite way than the strip above.

Cut slits down a star. Weave short strips across the top and bottom points.

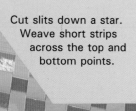

4. Continue weaving shorter and shorter strips of paper until you have filled the bottom part of the heart.

The orange strips woven through this star were cut in different widths.

5. To fill the top of the heart, cut four short strips of paper. Weave them at a slight angle, like this.

6. When the heart is completely filled, trim the ends off the strips, a little way away from the edges of the heart.

These flowers may
look complicated,
but they are easy
to paint.

244

Painted flowers

COLORED ART PAPER OR BRISTOL PAPER

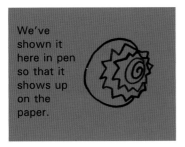

We've shown it here in pen so that it shows up on the paper.

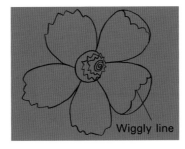

Wiggly line

1. Use a pencil to draw an oval for the middle of a flower. Add a spiral at one side and two wavy circles around it.

2. Add petals around the middle. To make them look as if they are curled over, draw a wiggly line inside the petal.

3. Add a long stem. Then, draw several leaves, making one of them look as if its end is curling over, like this.

Don't paint the parts that curl over.

4. Mix some white paint with just a little water. Then, use a thin paintbrush to paint over all your pencil lines.

5. Starting at the middle of the flower, paint a line out to the edge of a petal. Then, paint more lines to fill each petal.

If you don't have white paint, use a colored paint on white paper.

6. Paint a line down the middle of each leaf. Then, fill them with lots of lines. Fill in the stem completely with white.

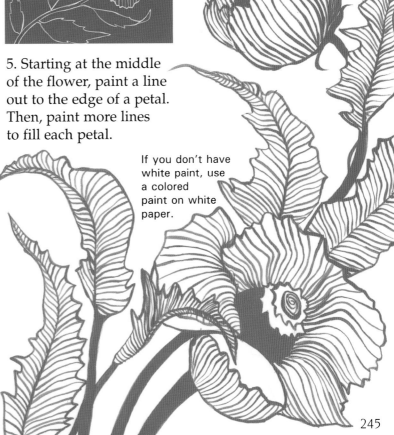

Colorful windows

CREAM OR ANOTHER PALE COLOR OF PAPER

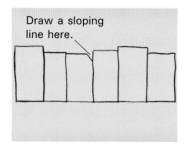

1. Draw several rectangles across the middle of the paper with a dip pen and black ink, or a felt-tip pen.

2. Draw simple patterns for roof tiles on some of the buildings. Add some chimneys and antennae.

3. Draw windows and doors. Copy some of the styles of windows from the big picture below.

Place your picture against a window. The light will glow through the tissue paper.

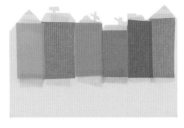

4. Use a craft knife to cut roughly around the top of the buildings. Cut out the windows, too.

5. Cut strips of tissue paper the width of each building and tape them to the back of the picture.

6. Turn the picture over and glue a piece of light blue tissue paper along the bottom for a canal.

You could draw some striped posts on the canal.

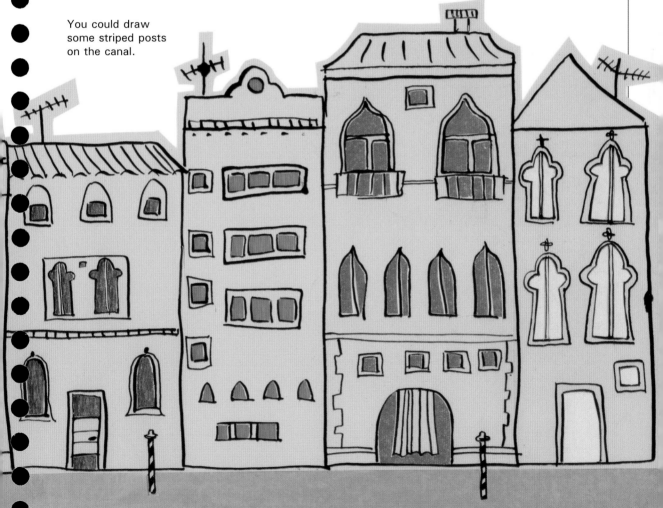

247

Sparkling squares
TRANSPARENT BOOK COVERING FILM

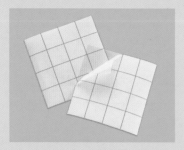

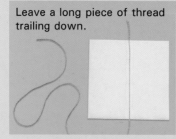

Leave a long piece of thread trailing down.

1. Cut two squares of book covering film, the same size. Peel the backing paper off one of them and lay it sticky-side up.

2. Cut a long piece of colored thread and lay it across the film, like this. It will stick to the sticky surface.

The shapes sparkle as they turn.

3. Rip lots of small pieces of tissue paper. Then, press them onto the film, leaving spaces in between them.

4. Press different shapes of sequins into the gaps between the paper. You could add some pieces of ribbon or thread, too.

Lay the thread on the film at different angles.

5. Peel the backing paper off the other piece of film and press it over the decorated piece. Then, trim the edges.

6. Attach more squares of book film below the first one, leaving some thread showing between the squares.

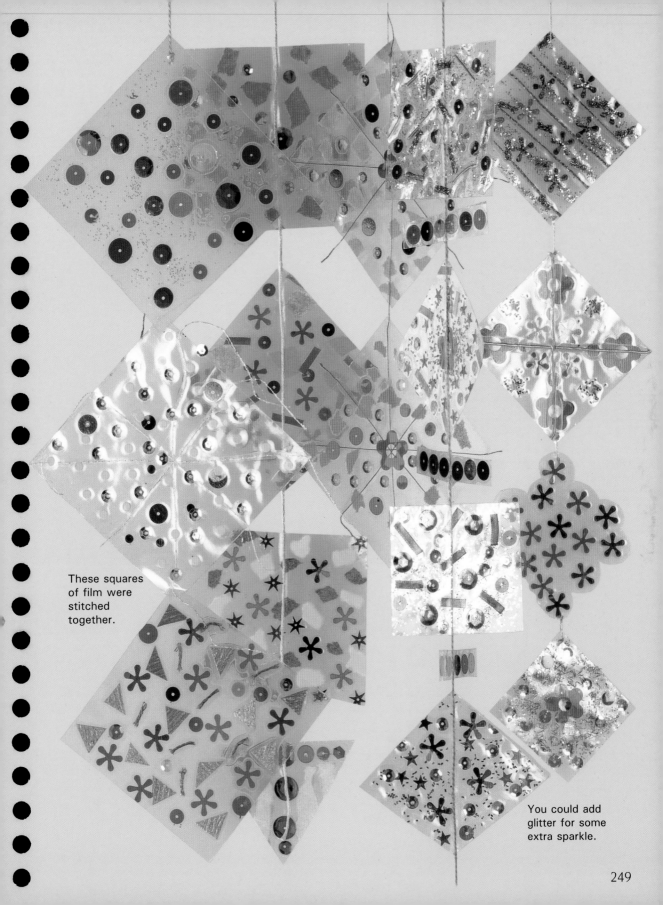

These squares
of film were
stitched
together.

You could add
glitter for some
extra sparkle.

249

Collage book covers

SHADES OF CREAM AND LIGHT BROWN PAPER

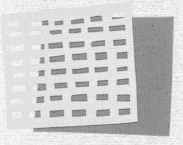

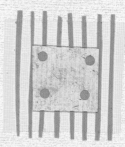

1. Use a craft knife to cut rows of little rectangles into a square of cream paper. Glue it onto a square of darker paper.

2. Then, use scissors to cut lots of thin strips of light brown paper and glue them onto a square of cream paper.

3. Use a hole puncher to punch holes into a paper square. Glue it onto brown paper, then glue them both on top of the strips.

The cream paper used in these squares is wallpaper.

Trim here. ————

4. Cut a 'spiral' in a paper square. Glue it at an angle onto some darker paper. Then, trim off any paper that overlaps the edge.

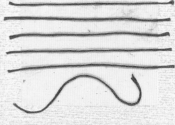

You could use these for the cover of a diary or photo album.

5. Cut several pieces of thick thread. Paint them with white glue, then press them in lines across a paper square.

6. Decorate another square with circles from a hole puncher. Then, decorate one more using the ideas shown below.

7. Cut a piece of paper to the height of the book you want to cover. Make it long enough to fold inside the cover.

8. Lay the decorated squares in the middle of the book cover. Glue them on with strong glue, then leave it to dry.

More ideas

Include a square from a scrap of handmade paper, if you have any.

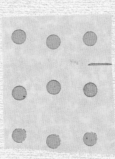

Fold some paper several times, then punch lines of holes in it.

Cut squares of different sizes and glue them on top of each other.

Add a small piece of paper weaving (see pages 240-241).

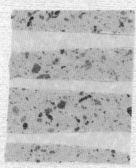

Cut strips of patterned paper and glue them on.

Rip strips of paper and glue them on top of each other.

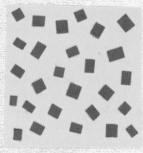

Glue on lots of little paper squares at different angles.

Pierce lots of holes with an old ballpoint pen or a blunt needle.

3-D cityscape

THIN WHITE CARDBOARD

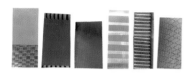

Make them roughly the same width.

1. For the buildings, cut rectangles of patterned paper from magazines. Glue them onto a strip of thin white cardboard.

2. Cut out and glue on a roof for each building. Make some of them pointed and others flat on top.

3. Cut out windows, chimneys and doors, and glue them on. Try to find paper with squared or lined patterns on them.

4. For the road, cut strips of blue shades of paper. Glue them on in front of the buildings. Add white lines, too.

5. To protect your collage and make it stronger, you could cover it with clear book covering film, but you don't have to.

6. Use a craft knife to cut around the buildings and the road. Leave a border of white cardboard around them.

Bend it between your fingers and thumbs.

7. To curve the street so that it stands up, hold it in the middle. Move your hands outward, bending it slightly as you go.

8. Make more streets in the same way. Make one without a road in front, then others which are taller than the first street.

9. Cut out metallic-looking papers for skyscrapers. Make them from several pieces of paper glued on top of each other.

Finish the cityscape with a road and hedges.

Assemble the streets one behind the other. You could press a small piece of poster tack on the back to secure them.

253

Dip pen drawings

BRISTOL PAPER OR LIGHT-COLORED ART PAPER

Try drawing modern and old-fashioned cars.

This red chalk pastel was smudged with a fingertip.

When you draw with a dip pen, it gives you a slightly uneven line.

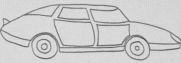

1. Pressing lightly, draw a simple outline of a car with a pencil. You could use pictures from books or magazines for reference.

2. Draw the windows, doors, wheels and hubcaps. Then, add the headlights and rear lights, then the bumpers.

If you don't have a dip pen, you could use a fountain pen.

3. Dip the nib of a dip pen into some ink and go over the pencil lines. Dip the pen into the ink each time the nib runs dry.

4. Add details such as door handles, side-view mirrors, radiator grills and license plates. Leave the ink to dry completely.

Leave some parts of the cars uncolored.

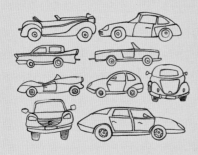

5. Draw lots more cars from different views. Do some from the side, some head-on and some from the back.

6. When the ink is completely dry, use chalk pastels or felt-tip pens to fill in different parts on each of the cars.

You could also use this technique to draw fashion accessories.

Draw clutch bags and shoulder bags.

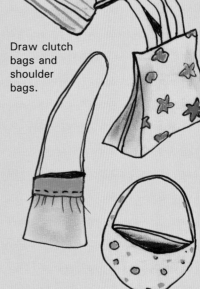

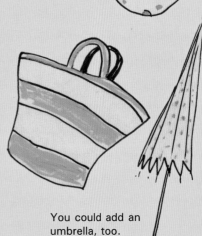

You could add an umbrella, too.

Frames

On the next four pages you can find out how to make different types of frames for your pictures.

When you make a frame, choose a color that will go well with the picture you are framing. If you decide to decorate your frame, don't make it too elaborate, otherwise your picture will be swamped by the patterns and colors.

This simple frame was made from strips of colored corrugated cardboard.

Simple strip frame

1. Cut a piece of cardboard the size you want your frame to be. Glue your picture in the middle of it.

2. Cut two strips of cardboard for the top and bottom of the frame. Make sure they overlap your picture a little.

3. For the sides of the frame, cut two pieces of cardboard that fit between the top and bottom strips.

4. Glue on the top strip of cardboard, then the two sides and finally the bottom strip to complete the frame.

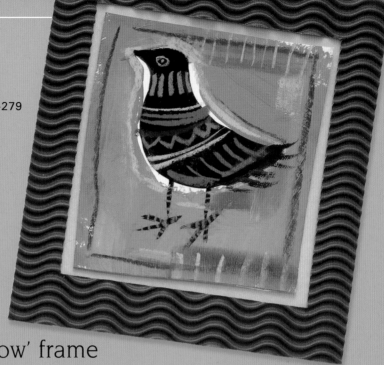

Look on pages 278-279 to draw and paint a bird like this.

It's often a good idea to leave a plain border between the edge of your picture and the frame.

A square 'window' frame

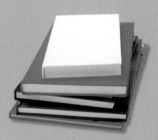

1. Cut two squares of cardboard the size you want the frame. Then, lay your picture on one of the squares.

2. Use a pencil to draw around your picture. This will give you a guide for the size for the 'window' you'll cut into the frame.

3. Draw another shape about ¼inch inside the pencil lines. Then, place the cardboard on an old magazine.

4. Cut along the inside shape with a craft knife. Cut each line several times rather than trying to cut through the first time.

5. Lay the frame over your picture. Turn them over and attach the picture with pieces of tape. Then, erase any pencil lines.

6. Glue the frame onto the spare cardboard square. Put a heavy pile of books on top until the glue has dried.

More frame ideas

These two pages show ideas for decorating the strip frame and window frame shown on the previous two pages.

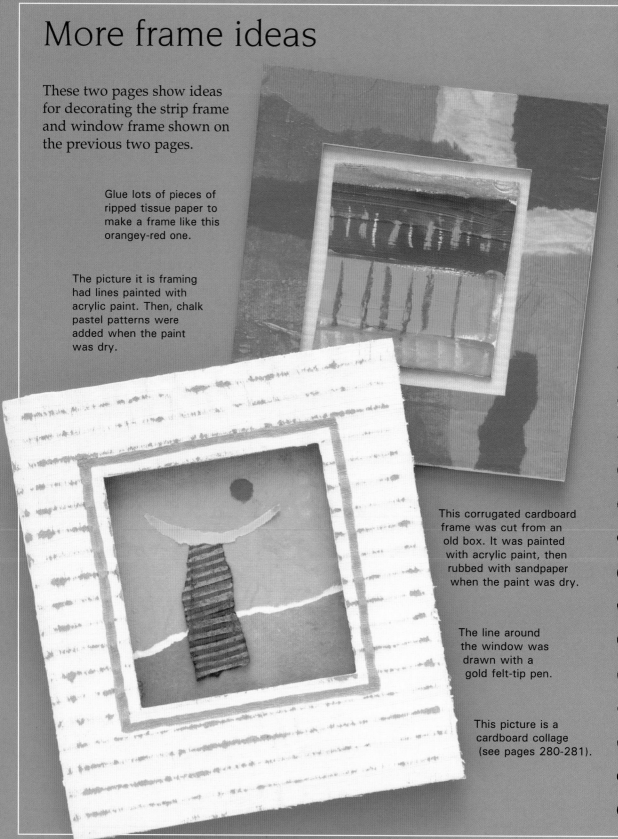

Glue lots of pieces of ripped tissue paper to make a frame like this orangey-red one.

The picture it is framing had lines painted with acrylic paint. Then, chalk pastel patterns were added when the paint was dry.

This corrugated cardboard frame was cut from an old box. It was painted with acrylic paint, then rubbed with sandpaper when the paint was dry.

The line around the window was drawn with a gold felt-tip pen.

This picture is a cardboard collage (see pages 280-281).

The strip frame above was made from a foil food tray. The patterns were drawn on the back with a ballpoint pen.

The middle frame was decorated with squares cut from pieces of textured paper (see pages 212-213).

The bottom frame was made using a foil food tray and decorated with squares of textured paper.

Ideas for hanging pictures

Bend this side upward.

For a loop hanger, cut a piece of thin string and use a piece of strong tape to attach it to the back of your frame.

For a metal hanger, unbend the end of a paperclip. Use several pieces of strong tape to attach it to the frame.

To make a stand, cut a triangle from cardboard and fold it in half. Cut the bottom edges at an angle, then glue on one half.

Scratching paint

WHITE CARDBOARD

1. Use a thick paintbrush to paint a piece of white cardboard with white acrylic paint. Leave it to dry completely.

2. Mix blue, green and black acrylic paint to make dark blue. Use it to paint a stripe, 1½inch wide, on top of the white paint.

The outline doesn't have to be too perfect.

3. While the paint is still wet, use the end of a paintbrush to scratch a simple feather shape. You need to work quickly.

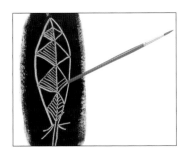

4. Use the end of a thin paintbrush, or a craft knife, to scratch zigzags down the feather. Scratch lines inside some the shapes.

You can paint on a color instead of white at step 1. This blue was painted on top of pink.

Draw the second feather upside down.

For a scratched painting, like these sunflowers, put yellow paint on top of orange.

5. Paint another stripe of blue paint touching the first one. Scratch a feather into the stripe in the same way.

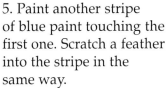

The outline of this cat was scratched first, then the patterns were added.

6. Continue painting and scratching until you have a row of feathers. Scratch a different pattern into each feather.

Try scratching an imaginary animal.

Paint a patch of color then scratch lines to make a grid. Quickly fill each one with a different pattern before the paint dries.

Fashion cut-outs

COLORED ART PAPER

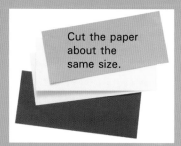
Cut the paper about the same size.

1. Cut out a page from an old magazine with a photograph or drawing of a figure wearing a shirt and pants.

2. Trace a simple outline of the head, body and clothes. Then, turn the tracing over and scribble pencil over the lines.

3. Cut two pieces of white paper, one brown piece and one pink. Make them larger than your figure drawing.

Press firmly.

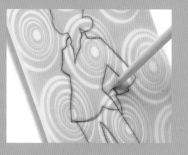

4. Lay the tracing, shaded-side down, onto the brown paper. Draw around the head, feet and hand with a ballpoint pen.

5. Cut them out with a craft knife, keeping all the shapes. Trace the shirt and pants onto the pink paper and cut them out.

6. Lay your tracing onto a piece of wrapping paper. Draw around the pants and shirt again, then cut them out.

7. Glue the large piece of brown paper onto one of the pieces of white paper. Glue the pink shirt and patterned pants on top.

8. Glue the patterned shirt onto the other piece of white paper. Then, glue the large piece of pink paper on top.

9. Then, glue the brown head, hand and feet onto the figure on the pink paper. (You don't use the pink pants at all).

Glue your pictures side by side on a large piece of paper.

If you can't find a suitable picture in a magazine, trace over one of these figures.

Oodles of doodles

WHITE PAPER OR BRISTOL PAPER

1. Paint lots of different shapes, like these, with red watercolor paint. Flick the bristles of the brush to spatter dots on top, too.

2. When the paint is dry, scribble around some of the shapes with a blue pencil. Add circles, lines and leaves in the spaces.

3. Start doodling lines, circles and dots over the top of the paint and pencil shapes, with a blue ballpoint pen.

4. Then, fill in the spaces between the shapes with lots of wavy lines, circles and squares. Add dots, stars and spirals, too.

5. Continue doodling around the shapes with the pen, so that you fill most of the paper with different patterns.

6. Then, turn some of the shapes into birds by adding legs, beaks, wings and feathers. Turn some shapes into flowers, too.

You could fill some of the spaces with scribbled blue pencil.

Embossed circles

THIN CARDBOARD AND ART PAPER

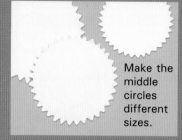

Make the middle circles different sizes.

1. Use a pair of compasses to draw three circles on a piece of thin cardboard. Make each one a slightly different size.

2. Draw a wavy edge around each circle and a plain circle in the middle of each one. Cut around the wavy lines.

3. In the middle of the largest circle, draw curved shapes. Then, carefully use a craft knife to cut them out.

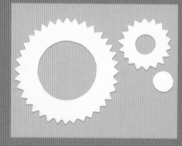

4. Use a hole puncher to punch holes in some scraps of cardboard. Open the puncher and glue the circles around the edge.

5. Cut the middle out of one of the other circles and cut a wavy line around it. Then, cut a circle out of its middle.

7. Glue another wavy-edged circle onto the remaining circle. Cut out a ring of cardboard and glue it in the middle.

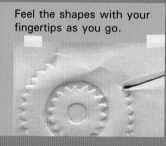

Feel the shapes with your fingertips as you go.

7. Lay all the pieces onto some paper or cardboard. Arrange them in an overlapping pattern, then glue them on.

8. Tape a piece of art paper over the circles. Use the end of a teaspoon to press and rub around the cardboard shapes.

9. Continue pressing around the shapes until you have revealed all the shapes. This technique is called 'embossing'.

Cut a window
frame (see page
257) and tape
your embossed
paper to the back.

This picture was embossed
onto silver art paper.

Fast food collage

PIECES OF PAPER TEXTURED WITH PAINT (SEE PAGES 212-213)

Add black marks on the bun.

1. Glue a piece of blue paper and a piece of textured paper across a large rectangle of purple paper, like this.

2. Cut two rectangles of checked paper from an old magazine, or draw some with felt-tip pens. Glue them at the top.

3. For the burger bun, cut two orange shapes from textured paper. Cut an oval for the burger and two shapes for tomatoes.

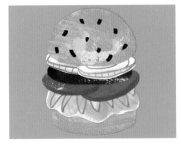

Cut the straw in two and glue it on at an angle.

4. Draw slices of onion with a blue pencil. Fill them in with blue paint. Draw some green lettuce, too. Cut out the shapes.

5. Glue the lettuce onto the bottom bun shape. Then, glue on the tomatoes, burger, onion, then the top bun shape.

6. For the drink, cut out a cup shape. Glue on a white oval and a smaller oval inside, for the drink. Paint a striped straw.

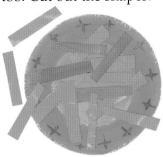

Cut out a foil lid for the carton.

7. Cut a circle from green paper. Then, paint a lighter green circle in the middle. Glue on orangey-yellow strips for the french fries.

8. Draw a plastic carton on a piece of white paper. Paint a red oval inside for the ketchup. Glue on a french fry.

9. Glue all the things you have made onto the large piece of paper. Add other things, such as silverware, muffins and napkins.

Fish and shrimp

DARK BLUE PAPER

1. Mix red and white poster paint or gouache to make pink. Paint two curved brushstrokes with a thick paintbrush.

This fish was painted with one short and one long wavy brushstroke.

2. When the paint is dry, use a white pencil to outline the brushstrokes. Add several lines for the fins and the tail.

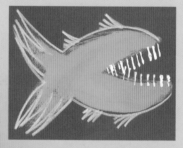

3. Dip the end of a piece of thin cardboard into thick white paint, then print a row of teeth on each jaw.

4. Mix some paler pink paint, then fingerprint lots of spots. Fingerprint a white eye. Add a black dot when the paint is dry.

Shrimp

1. Dip a thick paintbrush into red paint. Paint a curved brushstroke, lifting your brush up quickly at the end.

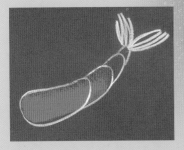

2. When the paint is dry, draw around the painted body with a white pencil. Add some more body segments and a tail.

3. Draw several lines at the top of the body for feelers. Then, add two very long lines, curving outward.

4. Draw several short curved lines along the body for the legs. Then, add an eye with a black felt-tip pen.

271

Inky beetles

BRISTOL PAPER OR THICK WHITE PAPER

1. Use ink to paint a large frame. When it's dry, draw an oval with an orange chalk pastel.

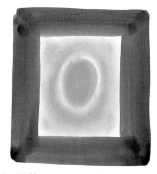

2. Fill in around the oval with blue pastel. Then, use a finger to smudge the pastel over the paper.

3. Dip a thin paintbrush or dip pen into some pink ink and use it to draw a simple outline of a beetle.

4. Add eyes and feelers to the head. Draw 'toes' at the end of the legs. Add patterns on the wings.

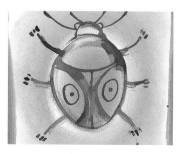

5. While the ink is still wet, smudge it across the the body and along the legs with a fingertip.

6. Put your picture onto a newspaper. Then, flick a paintbrush to splatter ink over the beetle.

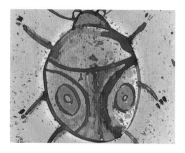

7. Fill in parts on the head, wings and body with a gold pen. Draw pastel dots on the wings.

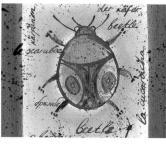

8. Use a dip pen and ink or a thin felt-tip pen to write around the beetle. Use flowing lettering.

9. Smudge the pastel dots on the body. Then, use pastels and a gold pen to decorate the frame.

Robot

THICK CARDBOARD

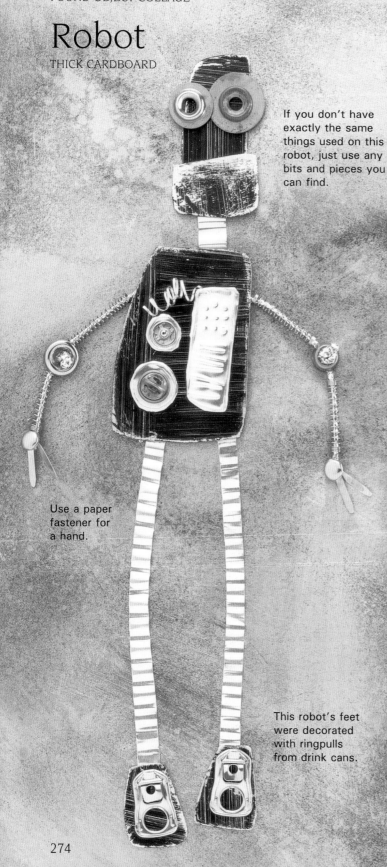

If you don't have exactly the same things used on this robot, just use any bits and pieces you can find.

Use a paper fastener for a hand.

This robot's feet were decorated with ringpulls from drink cans.

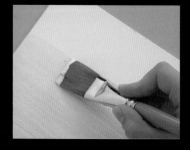

1. For the background, paint a piece of thick cardboard with silver paint. Then, leave it to dry completely.

Rub the paint around and around.

2. Use a paper towel to wipe purple paint on top of the silver. Then, use a clean paper towel to rub off some of the paint.

Paint the matt side of a piece of foil if you don't have a lid.

3. Meanwhile, mix purple and black paint together. Paint it onto the foil lid of a food tray. Paint it so some brushmarks show.

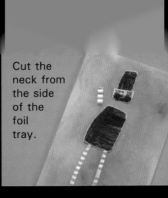

Cut the neck from the side of the foil tray.

4. Cut the bottom and one side from a foil food tray. Then, cut two long strips from the side for the robot's legs.

5. Cut a body, a head, mouth and feet from the painted lid. Lay them on the background along with the legs. Cut out a neck.

Use springs from old ballpoint pens.

Knot

6. Cut a piece of thread for the arms and tie a knot halfway along it. Push the ends through a washer, then two springs.

7. Glue all the pieces onto the background. Glue the mouth on the head and add two washers for each eye.

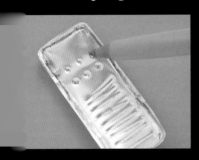

You could add a press stud or the back of a badge.

8. Cut a rectangle from the foil tray. Draw shapes on it with a ballpoint pen, then turn it over and glue it onto the body.

9. Cut a very thin strip from the edge of the foil tray. It will curl as you cut it. Glue it onto the body, along with some foil circles.

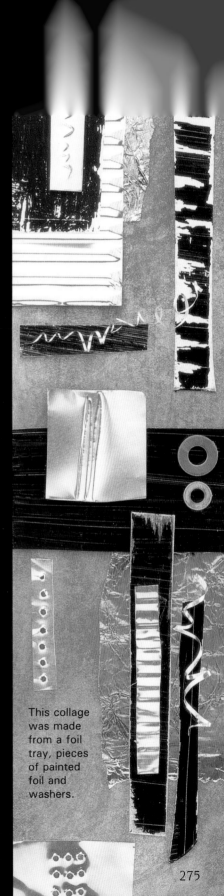

This collage was made from a foil tray, pieces of painted foil and washers.

Pink landscape

WHITE CARDBOARD

Use acrylic paint.

1. Stir yellow and orange paint together so that they are roughly mixed. Paint curves on some cardboard. Add pink curves on top.

2. Roughly mix darker yellow and orange paint. Paint two hills across the middle of the cardboard and fill in below them.

3. When the paint is dry, mix two shades of deep pink paint. Brush them in two lines across the bottom of the landscape.

In this landscape some trees were added with an orange oil pastel.

276

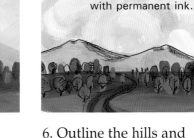

4. For the trees, dab lots of vertical brushmarks in deep pink along the bottom of the hills. Add some purple trees, too.

5. Paint a purple curve for a road. Make it get gradually wider toward the bottom. Leave the paint to dry completely.

6. Outline the hills and some trees with a black felt-tip pen. Then, add some shading to them with a black oil pastel.

Use a felt-tip pen with permanent ink.

You could add small farm buildings, like the ones below, to give your landscape a sense of scale.

Striped and spotted birds

BROWN WRAPPING PAPER

1. Draw three squares on a piece of brown wrapping paper. Then, draw a simple outline of a bird in each square.

2. Paint one bird with pink paint. Put just a little black paint on your brush and fill in the square so that some paper shows.

3. Paint one of the other birds in black and one with pale orange. Paint their backgrounds blue and dark brown.

4. When the paint is completely dry, draw a square around the pink bird with a blue chalk pastel. Add some shapes.

5. Add legs and feet, and outline the body with a pale chalk pastel. Then, add bright pink lines on the bird and in the square.

6. Use a dip pen and black ink, or a black felt-tip pen, to add an eye, lines on the body and a beak. Paint some black spots, too.

These birds were painted and drawn in the same way as the steps, but had more patterns added in the background.

7. Draw chalk pastel lines around the black bird. Add a patch of purple on the left-hand side and smudge it a little.

8. Use different shades of blue pastels to draw an eye and markings. Add pastel stripes to the legs, feet and tail.

9. Draw patterns and markings on the orange bird with ink and pastels, as you did before. Then, decorate the background.

Cardboard collage

CARDBOARD AND TEXTURED PAPERS (SEE PAGES 212-213)

You could use corrugated cardboard.

1. Rip a rectangle of cardboard and one from paper, painted blue. Cut a rectangle from cardboard, then glue them together.

2. Rip triangular shapes from textured paper. Then, glue them on the top piece of cardboard, making a zigzag shape.

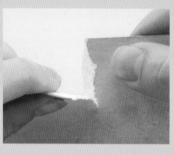

The ripped blue paper is under here.

3. Rip another rectangle of painted paper. Hold it in one hand and tear it up toward you. This gives a pale, ripped edge.

4. Glue on the painted rectangle, then glue pale tissue paper on top so that the ripped edges show. Add a blue dot.

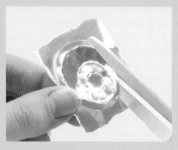

5. Rip two spirals in a piece of silver paper. Then, use scissors to cut beside the ripped edges to make thin spiral strips.

6. Glue the silver spirals onto the painted paper. Then, rip a rectangle from red paper and glue it beside them.

This collage was made using corrugated cardboard and a variety of textured paper.

The corrugated cardboard above was cut from an old box. The top layer of paper was pulled off to reveal the ridges.

This black paper was from photocopied paper.

7. Glue a black rectangle across the bottom of the cardboard and glue a strip of paper, ripped from a magazine, on top.

8. Rip a blue rectangle and an orange circle from textured paper. Glue them on, wrapping any spare paper around to the back.

9. Rip a thin strip of black paper. Glue it on so that it overlaps the red stripe, the blue rectangle and the tissue paper above.

Watercolor city

THICK WHITE PAPER OR CARDBOARD

You could paint a taller building above the row of buildings at step 1.

These tiny people make the buildings look huge.

1. Mix different shades of orange, purple and red watercolor paint. Paint a row of buildings, almost touching each other.

2. Mix some light blue watercolor and paint the sky above the buildings. Add darker blue shapes when the sky has dried.

3. Use ink and a dip pen, or a felt-tip pen, to outline the buildings at the front in black. Draw a roof on each one.

Some of the windows in this picture were filled in roughly with ink.

4. Draw windows and doors on the buildings. Then, add extra details such as shop windows and awnings.

5. Outline the buildings at the back. Make them look like skyscrapers by adding rows of dots and lines for windows.

6. Draw some sidewalks. Then, paint simple shapes for cars and outline them when the paint is dry. Draw some people, too.

More ideas

Over the next four pages there are lots more ideas using the techniques found in this book. Turn back to the pages which are mentioned to find out how they were done.

The birds above were fingerprinted (see pages 230-231).

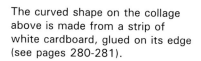

The collage below was made from pieces of dyed paper (see pages 218-219).

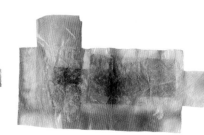

The curved shape on the collage above is made from a strip of white cardboard, glued on its edge (see pages 280-281).

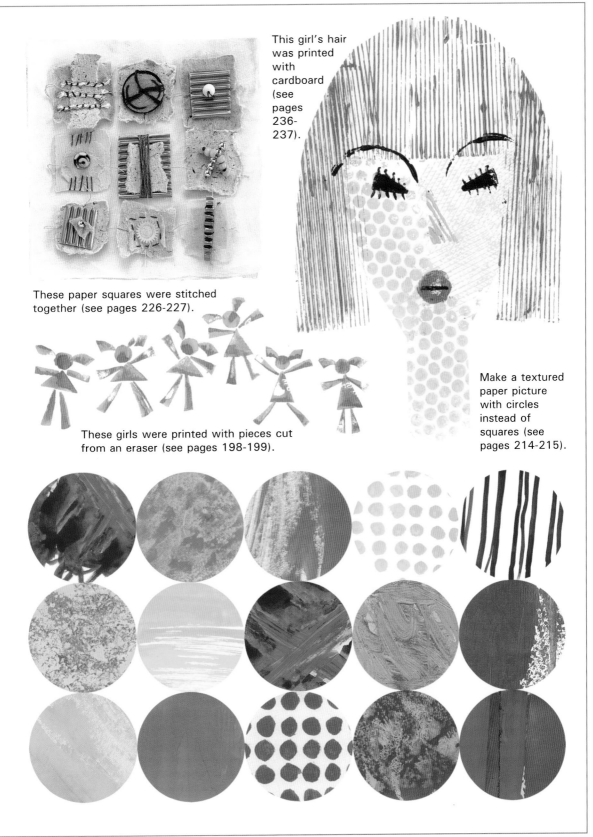

This girl's hair was printed with cardboard (see pages 236-237).

These paper squares were stitched together (see pages 226-227).

These girls were printed with pieces cut from an eraser (see pages 198-199).

Make a textured paper picture with circles instead of squares (see pages 214-215).

Use the punched hole technique (see pages 206-207) for decorating trees and houses.

The head and body of this crocodile have been woven with paper strips (see pages 242-243).

These flowers were painted using the same technique as the frogs on pages 204-205.

This frog and bugs' collage was made from pieces of textured paper (see pages 220-221).

Make a face following the steps on page 208, then add patterns on the sweater with white paint.

The reptile below was decorated using the steps on pages 278-279.

Use bits and pieces to make a collage of a dog (see pages 274-275).

This tissue paper flower had long individual running stitches sewn through the middle (see page 224).

Index

Acknowledgements

Every effort has been made to trace the copyright holders of the material in this book. If any rights have been omitted, the publishers offer their sincere apologies and will rectify this in any subsequent edition following notification. The publishers are grateful to the following organisations and individuals for their contributions and permission to reproduce material. Page 116 Vincent van Gogh 'Olive Orchard with Mountains' © Francis G. Mayer/CORBIS. Page 130 J.M.W. Turner 'Rain, Steam, and Speed - The Great Western Railway' © National Gallery, London. Page 146 Waves © Digital Vision. Page 160 Guanacos - Ian Jackson.